Complete Book of
Defensive Line
Play

COMPLETE BOOK OF DEFENSIVE LINE PLAY

Joe Giampalmi

Parker Publishing Company, Inc.
West Nyack, N.Y.

Library of Congress Cataloging in Publication Data

Giampalmi, Joseph
   Complete book of defensive line play.

   Includes index.
   1. Football--Defense. 2. Football coaching.
I. Title.
GV951.18.G5   796.33'22   78-23670
ISBN 0-13-156158-8

Printed in the United States of America

God has been good to me. He gave me Madeline, Joey, Jeff, Lisa, Mom and Dad. And thanks to them, I give you *Complete Book of Defensive Line Play*.

Developing Your Defensive Linemen

Complete Book of Defensive Line Play offers you a comprehensive analysis of all facets of defensive line play. It begins where a good defensive lineman must begin, with a good stance and quick start, and ends where a lot of games are often decided, with someone gaining an advantage from being aware of a certain rule. Between starts and finishes are: eight initial defensive charges; four popular pass rush techniques; keys to recognizing game-breaking plays; techniques for developing defensive ends and interior linemen; methods of getting linemen to where they can make the tackle; adjustments for specific offensive sets; and preparation for any unusual opportunity that is presented.

This book gives you the opportunity to get maximum mileage out of your average and below average linemen. The greatest satisfaction that you, as coaches, can get is developing good players from average and below average players. When you aren't blessed with superstars, you have to work harder to perfect the skills and techniques that are natural to the All-Americans.

This book also gives you the ingredients for making an average defensive lineman good and a good defensive lineman excellent. Well-skilled defensive linemen are the equalizers to physically superior offensive linemen. Your defensive linemen will have a better chance to beat their man if they can get a pass or run key by reading a hand, elbow, or heel. Similarly, your defensive line will beat the offensive line off the ball if they watch and move on the movement of the fingers of the offensive linemen.

You will see how the application of a principle of physics, the inclined plane, will help you win the most critical collision in football—the one-on-one. You have all watched films of two good linemen trying to control each other at the line of scrimmage by trying to force the other back. You are asking them to push back a force of nearly 300 pounds. If you have them use the inclined plane principle, then you are reducing considerably the weight of that force.

The unique features of this book make it different from other books written on the subject. All situations involving defensive line play are covered: run, pass, short yardage, long yardage, kicking downs, loose balls, unusual weather, unusual formations, two-minute defense, equalizing match-ups, and so forth.

The idiosyncrasies of all defensive line positions are discussed. Whether your defense plays head, gap, shoulder, even or odd, there is something for you. Chapter 4 tells you how to put a safety valve into your defensive line play that will protect your defense against a bootleg.

During the closing minutes of a close game, you demand an extra effort from your players. Likewise, you owe them an extra effort on your part. You must prepare your defense to do everything possible in the last few minutes—whether you're losing or winning. Chapters 10 and 11 cover both situations.

In Chapter 10 you'll see how to cause a fumble by placing a hand in the area where the ball is least protected—the back point just below the elbow. And in Chapter 11 you'll get specific defensive assignments for playing "two-minute defense"—an area of defense that is frequently overlooked.

Chapter 6 shows you tested methods for coaching your linemen to recognize special plays. Your defensive linemen will learn to anticipate screens when you teach them to react to:

1. Their charge not being slowed down

2. The quarterback dropping back extra deep
3. Seeing a back slide out into the flat

You can also alert them to screen situations by being aware that most screens are thrown on second or third downs when twelve or more yards are needed for the first down. Many teams like to throw a screen immediately following a fifteen yard penalty. This same chapter also discusses keys to recognizing a type of screen that has become popular in recent years—the middle screen.

Similar keys are given to help your linemen anticipate draws, traps, and counters. Chapter 9 gives you individual adjustments to compensate for the strengths of specific offenses. You all have problems defending different kinds of options because you have to stretch your defense to defend three running areas on the same side. Your having to defend three running areas does not mean you have to defend them evenly. One of the three runners you are defending is usually weaker than the other two—frequently the quarterback. When you defend the option, you commonly play man to man, but you should avoid playing your strongest defender on your opponent's weakest runner.

You will also get guidelines for individual plays against the Pro and the Wing T. In addition, Chapter 9 will tell you adjustments that you can make on the goal line.

At the conclusion of each chapter, drills are given specifically for the skills and techniques in that chapter. The drills follow the same sequence as the chapter.

Finally, you are given one of the easiest methods of gaining an advantage over your opposing coach—knowledge of the rule book. Defensive linemen should know what constitutes off-sides and encroachment. They should know that they are allowed to make contact with the punter if they get a piece of the ball. They should know the difference between a forward pass and a backward pass, and that they are permitted to advance a backward pass. Rules that can improve your defensive line play are discussed in Chapter 12.

In conclusion, this book offers you everything you need to make your defensive linemen as diversified as possible. The tested techniques will make your average linemen good and your good linemen excellent, and these techniques discussed are in relation to the various defenses that you may be using.

                                                    J.G.

Acknowledgments

God has been good to me. He has blessed me with people who have guided me and have given me opportunities. I would like to mention some of these people.

C.D. Donato, my first football coach, made football fun when I was a young "O."

My high school coaches, who would never let me be an "X," helped me fulfill my childhood dream of playing football for St. James High School. Mr. Francis "Bean" Brennan and Joe Logue taught me perseverance—the most valuable lesson I learned in school.

At P.M.C. (Widener College) the late Lee "Rock" Royer, George Hansel and Jim Komernicki taught me to believe and perform what I didn't think I could do. They also prepared me to coach.

Bob Fithian, my head coach for fourteen years, gave me the opportunity to do what others prepared me for. Our years together have produced more fun than wins—and the wins approach a hundred.

I also enjoyed the assistant coaches I've worked with: Jim McFadden, Tom Walters, Fran Tracy, Allan Brewster and recently Tom Kent.

The present assistants at Sun Valley are good coaches, but better friends. I sincerely thank Mike Lashendock, Bill Benedict and Ron Withelder.

Other people who had a direct influence on this book include: John Mooney, Harry Chaykum, Dottie Reynolds and Herman Masin.

I also owe thanks to the Delaware County Football Coaches' Association and the Chester Chapter of the PIAA Football Officials.

In addition, I would like to thank Dave Bove for creating the illustrations and Lori Panzulo and Diane DiOrio for their help typing.

I would also like to thank the Penn-Delco School District, my administrators at Sun Valley (Charley Fitzgerald, Ken Bolyard and Dick Miller) and the young men who were educated at Sun Valley and played defense for me.

I am indebted to the defensive linemen of Sun Valley who gave up an average of 4.4 points per game (when they were on the field) and won for us our fourth Philadelphia Suburban II Championship in the last five years. I rate them the best defensive team I ever coached. Thank you Roger Searfass, Ed Lanciano, Dave Christopher, John April, Matt Serge and Pat Masternardo. We laughed a lot, cried a little and won a lot.

Contents

1

Coaching Stance
and Starts
for Defensive Linemen

Starting with a good stance. Looking for keys. Varying alignment but not assignment. Advantages of 3- and 4-point stances. Adjusting to shifting offenses. Moving on movement.

Starting with a Good Stance

If William Shakespeare were a football coach, he would have said, "All that ends well, must begin well."

If you would like to be as successful as Shakespeare, you must do everything possible to insure that your defensive linemen do everything right at the beginning of the play. Your defensive linemen must begin every play with a good stance and a quick start.

A good defensive stance is not a comfortable position. If it were comfortable, you would see more people going around on

17

threes and all fours. A good defensive stance must be more functional than comfortable. Your defensive linemen must use a stance that enables them to successfully execute their basic responsibilities, which are:

1. Neutralize the charge of the opponent.
2. Control the assigned area.
3. Release from the opponent and get to the ball carrier.

The essentials of a functional stance are the proper positioning of the following:

1. Head
2. Back
3. Angles at the ankles, knees, and hips

The most important part of the body in all sports is the head. This applies not only to the use of what is in the head but also to where the head is located. The head establishes the alignment that the remainder of the body follows. The back and the vertical angles at the ankles, knees, and hips cannot be properly located unless the head is correctly positioned.

If your lineman has his head too low, his tail will be too high, causing his back to be on a downward angle and extending the hip angle, which will cause a reduction of thrust when a charge is made. If he has his head too high, his tail will be forced down, causing his back to angle upward and reducing the critical hip angle. This also causes a reduction of thrust.

The head is at the proper angle when there is a slight bend behind the neck and the back is parallel to the ground. (See Figure 1-1.) The back must be parallel and arched. This position allows maximum upper body strength on contact and provides maximum force directed through the opponent. If your lineman has his back angled down, his force will be directed into the ground. If his back is pointed up, he will make contact too high.

When the back and head are positioned correctly, the critical angles at the ankles, knees, and hips will be properly aligned. The quick extension of these angles provides the thrust that is an

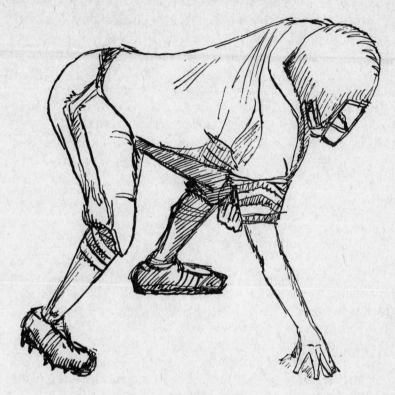

Figure 1-1

essential part of winning the most critical collision in football—
the one-on-one.

Looking for Keys

A good stance will become natural with repetition, and it
will require very little thought. Your defensive linemen can use
their thinking to read keys and anticipate situations.

From the time the last play ends to the time the next play
begins, your linemen should be looking for indications of upcom-
ing situations. Before going into the defensive huddle, they
should survey field position (including hash mark), down and
distance, score, time, wind, and so forth.

After the defensive huddle, your linemen should watch the offensive linemen break the huddle. Train your players to look for offensive linemen who are communicating. These opponents are likely to be involved in a critical part of the play. Your linemen may also observe offensive men looking for their assigned defender. Offensive linemen are more likely to look for their man if the location of the defender is constantly varying.

Your linemen can get additional keys from the stance and alignment of the opponent and from the overall offensive formation. Your linemen should be looking for keys that indicate:

    1. Run
    2. Pass
    3. Direction of the play

Defensive linemen should first be aware of any formation tendencies that are a key. Other keys come from observation of the alignment of their man. Your linemen should watch for variations in splits and depth that indicate:

    1. A pull for a quick pitch, sweep, or trap
    2. Stretching the backside away from a play that is going to the other side (see Figure 1-2.)

DIRECTION OF PLAY

Figure 1-2

    3. Tightening the side of the play to make a short outside corner (see Figure 1-3.)

DIRECTION OF PLAY

Figure 1-3

The hands and feet can offer additional keys. A lot of weight forward on the fingers or knuckles can indicate that the offensive man is going straight ahead for a run, while little weight forward and the fingers off the ground can indicate that the offensive man is going back to pass block.

Reading the feet in conjunction with the hands makes the key even more reliable. When the opponent's heels are on the ground and his weight is off his hand, the opponent is going to set up for a pass or he is going to come off the ball so slowly that your man will be able to control him no matter what the play.

Other pass keys shown by an offensive lineman are:

1. The head tilted back farther than usual
2. The tail lower than usual
3. The elbow bent so that he can push back

All these pass keys are shown in Figure 1-4.

Figure 1-4

Running plays can be anticipated by watching an opponent in his stance who:

1. Looks in the direction of his block
2. Points his head in the direction of his block.
3. Points a toe in the direction of his block.

The successful reading of a key depends on your linemen's total observation of his man and the recognition of the offensive alignment. The more factors that indicate a particular tendency, the more likely that the play will occur.

Varying Alignment, but Not Assignment

While your defensive lineman is observing his offensive man for keys, the offensive man is looking for keys to indicate what the defensive man will be doing. A defender who lines up in a different location for every play and who goes in a different direction on every play is the most difficult defender to block—ask your offensive linemen. Figure 1-5 shows some of the possible varying alignments for interior offensive linemen. Their assignment is to hit head-up in each alignment.

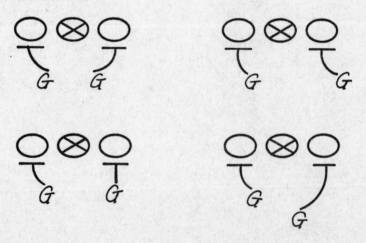

Figure 1-5

An offensive lineman has a feeling of security when the defender lines up in the same place and goes in the same direction, play after play. You can easily make an offensive lineman feel insecure by varying the alignment of your defensive linemen. Where they end up is more important than where they start.

Varying alignment is especially effective if you use a stunting defense. The key to successfully varying alignments in a stunting defense is to be back off the ball. This will allow your defender to get to his assigned area without getting cut off.

You should set limits to the area in which your linemen may vary their alignment. For example, a lineman who is assigned to hit his opponent's outside shoulder should align no farther than having his head outside the opponent's shoulder. (See Figure 1-6.)

Figure 1-6

In addition to making the offensive linemen feel insecure, varying alignment is likely to entice the quarterback to run plays into what appear to be natural holes in the defense. However, your opponent will not be running a percentage play, and the gap will quickly close at the snap of the ball.

There are two critical situations in which your linemen must not vary alignment: short yardage and the goal line. In these situations your linemen must fight to defend every inch. Those valuable inches will be jeopardized if your linemen are back off the ball and do not use a direct charge. In most other situations the offense will not be attempting to gain a few inches, so you will not endanger your defense by having your linemen off the ball and varying their alignment.

Adjusting to Shifting Offenses

Varying alignment can delay the offensive charge and shifting offenses can delay the defensive charge. The problem arises when your defensive linemen react to the offensive shift as if it were the snap.

This should not be a problem for your inside defenders who can see the full ball, but adjustments must be made for defenders who line up outside the middle area. These outside defenders can become easily confused when trying to distinguish between the offensive lineman (with his hands on his knees) moving down and the offensive lineman moving forward.

The key to recognizing the difference between the two is to watch the movement of the man's hands. When the offensive man moves his hands back, he will be moving forward and the defender should react. If the man's hands go down, he is shifting and the defender shouldn't react.

Not moving on a shift is contrary to teaching your defensive linemen to move on movement. Your preparation for a team that shifts should include many repetitions of your linemen seeing and reacting to the shifting moves and starting moves of offensive linemen.

You can have built-in protection against going off sides on a shift if you move your defensive linemen a yard off the ball. If you stunt or vary alignment, your linemen will already be back. Being off the ball will give your linemen a margin of error if they move on the wrong movement. If a lineman moves prematurely when the offensive man shifts, the one-yard cushion will prevent his being off sides. The defensive disadvantage of being off balance will be offset by the offensive man coming off the ball from the up position, which is extremely high for blocking. The lower lineman, the defender in this case, will have the advantage.

Advantages of 3- and 4-Point Stances

Both the 3- and 4-point stances enable your defensive linemen to come off the ball low and quickly. Each stance has its advantages. The criteria for which one a particular lineman chooses should be determined by the one that you can teach best and the one that enables him to perform best.

The traditional 3-point stance offers better mobility in all directions because the center of gravity is closer to its natural location—the feet. From this stance a lineman can quickly move to a running position to pursue the play. Also, the 3-point position permits a hand to be free to make use of the defensive advantage permitted by the rules.

An advantage of the 4-point stance is that it keeps linemen lower because they start lower. Keeping linemen lower, especially high school linemen, can be a problem, and the 4-point stance is a possible solution.

Tests have been performed to measure which stance is quicker. Our personal experience of measuring the quickness of both stances showed no measurable difference. However, since sprinters use a variation of the 4-point stance, we would conclude that the 4-point stance is quicker, but that doesn't necessarily mean it is better for defensive linemen.

We prefer the traditional 3-point stance because we know it better, and we believe that it offers more mobility for our stunting defenses. Also, when was the last time you have seen a professional lineman use a 4-point stance?

Both the 3-point and 4-point stances enable your defensive linemen to come off the ball low and quickly. Each stance has its advantages, and your linemen should use the one that enables them to perform best.

Moving on Movement

Whichever stance you choose, it must enable your defensive linemen to get off the ball as quickly as possible—on the first indication of offensive movement. The first movement by the offensive lineman is with his hand (both hands if he's using a 4-point stance). Your defensive linemen must concentrate on the hands of their man. A nose guard and other defensive middle men who are extremely close to the offensive center can easily see the complete ball and can move on the movement of the ball. Teaching your defensive linemen to move on the first sign of movement, the hand or the ball, can virtually eliminate your defense's being offsides.

Conditioning defensive linemen to move on movement can become a problem if they also play on offense. We train our offensive linemen to listen for sounds and our defensive linemen not to listen to sounds.

When drilling the defense, your linemen should never move on sound—either from a whistle or from a coach. During defensive drills that involve offensive linemen, the defender should not be told the starting count. Many one-on-one drills can be executed without a starting count by having the offensive man move when he is ready.

Problems sometimes occur with two-way performers when you are playing a team whose offense uses a starting count similar to your offense's starting count. Linemen who are conditioned to move on a particular sound on offense may move on that same sound when they are on defense.

If your linemen are having a problem with false movements during a game, you can temporarily correct the problem by moving them off the ball, similar to what you would do to correct premature moving when a team shifts. When your defensive linemen move on movement, they will be getting off the ball as quickly as possible and reducing the offense's advantage of knowing the starting count.

In conclusion, getting a good start is the first step you and your defensive linemen should take if you are going to successfully defend each play. A good start is: a good stance, an awareness of what the offense is likely to do, and moving when the offense moves. A good start is being mentally and physically prepared to encounter the most critical collision in football—the one-on-one.

Drills

The drills at the conclusion of each chapter are merely suggestions. We have used them successfully, and they are effective for our defensive philosophy. Some drills may benefit you; others may give you ideas for variations that are suited to your defensive play. Drills should meet the needs of the defense and the defensive players. Don't overlook the fact that sometimes defensive linemen need a drill that gives good plain fun—that's what our game is all about.

DRILLS

1. Find the Key.

Purpose: To develop recognition of keys.

Procedure: A line of offensive linemen face the defense. Each offensive man shows a different key. The defensive men walk past each man, identifying the key.

Comment: When the defensive linemen learn to recognize the offensive keys, they can learn to react to them in one-on-one drills.

2. One-on-One.

Purpose: There are many purposes of this drill. The needs for this drill in Chapter 1 are: reading and reacting to keys, varying alignment, adjusting to shifting offenses, and starting on movement.

Procedure: Two linemen, about a yard apart, face each other. The procedure is determined by the skill you want to drill.

Comment: We all use this basic drill as well as many variations of it. The importance of conditioning defensive linemen to move on movement and not sound cannot be overemphasized. Do not use this drill with the defense aware of the starting count. If you do, you will be conditioning your defensive linemen to go offsides. An effective technique that we use is to have both linemen set and then permit the offensive linemen to move when they wish. This simulates game conditions.

3. Ear Muff Drill.

Purpose: To condition defensive linemen to move on movement and not on sound.

Procedure: One, two, or three linemen line up on the coach, who is on one knee. The defensive linemen can react to either the movement of the coach's hand or to a ball in his hand.

Comment: The coach should try to distract the player's concentration by trying to get them to jump on cadence sounds and whistle sounds. Players should assume they are wearing ear muffs and disregard all sounds.

4. Traffic Light Drill.

Purpose: To develop a good stance and a quick start when linemen are extremely tired.

Procedure: All defensive linemen take their stance on the goal line or a similar line. On the hand movement of a coach, all linemen sprint 5 yards to the next line and reset in their stances.

Comment: This is a good conditioning drill to use at the end of practice when linemen are tired. Be prepared to correct the signs of a tired stance: head down, tail up, and back like a ski slope.

2

Winning the One-on-One with the Defense

Executing seven initial charges. Winning the stalemate. Applying the principle of the inclined plane. Equalizing uneven match-ups.

Your linemen need a good stance and a quick start before they make contact with their opponents. Good initial mechanics insures quickness and efficiency—necessities for all your linemen. They must have quickness and efficiency to make contact in the neutral zone or on the offensive side of the line of scrimmage. If contact is made on the defensive side, your defender must have superior strength to compensate for his lack of quickness.

When two linemen of equal or near equal ability make contact, they maintain a position called the stalemate—the collision of two equal forces. The proper technique after the stalemate is critical if your lineman is to control his opponent. He can gain control by applying a simple principle of physics—the inclined plane.

Executing Seven Initial Charges

After your linemen have mastered a good stance and a quick start, they must learn a series of charge techniques for making contact with the offense. When football was less complex, initial defensive charges were frequently overlooked. We used to instruct our linemen to "destroy your man and get to the ball." Today, defensive linemen need a complete repertoire of techniques to keep abreast with their offensive counterparts who are developing new techniques for option offenses.

There are seven common charge techniques that the defensive lineman can use. The purposes of the charge techniques are:

1. Neutralize the charge of the offensive man.
2. Control him.
3. Maintain a position where the defensive responsibilities can be executed.

The techniques that he masters depend on his physical assets as well as his defensive responsibilities.

The following sections explain and suggest a possible use of each charge for your defense. Not all charges are adaptable to all players and to all defenses. Also remember that you have more variability in changing your defense than you do in changing your defensive players.

1. Shoulder Lift

The first and most common defensive charge is the shoulder lift. The purpose of the charge is to quickly neutralize the offensive charge and maintain a position that allows control of the area on each side.

The charge is executed by firing the upper arm and shoulder into the opponent's chest, just above the numbers. (See

Figure 2-1

Figure 2-1.) The upper arm increases the shoulder surface and allows the defender maximum area with which to contact the opponent's chest. The blow, when the right shoulder is used, is delivered up through the front of the shoulder pads, slightly toward the opponent's right shoulder.

When the forearm is used to deliver a blow, the hitting surface of the arm can be strengthened by rolling the back of the wrist inward so that the palm is facing the opponent. This twisting movement tightens the forearm muscles which make contact with the offensive man. Immediately after contact with the striking arm and shoulder, the heel of the left hand is brought up under the man's shoulder pads and rapid force is applied to prevent that shoulder from turning, which would give blocking position to the offensive man.

The key to successfully executing the shoulder lift is coming off the ball with the tail slightly lower than the shoulders. This position allows the defender's shoulders to get under the opponent's shoulders. When the back is arched in this position, the lower body strength can be totally utilized. When the tail is low, the shoulders and back can work up at the proper angle.

The thrust of the blow comes mainly from the leg on the same side as the shoulder being used. On contact, the foot, knee, and hip angles are close to 90°. As the three angles straighten, the force is transmitted to the shoulder and arm. The force behind the blow is determined more by the strength of the leg than the strength of the shoulder.

The force of the leg and shoulder must be delivered through the opponent's numbers. If the force is delivered too high, the chest and midsection of the defensive man will easily be exposed to the blocker. If the force is too low, the defender will force himself to the ground. The opposite leg gives an initial push and then is used primarily for balance. It balances the thrust of the leg and the blow of the shoulder.

A common fault of the shoulder lift is the head being out near the opponent's arm. This allows the defender to control only one side of his man. It also places the opposite hand in a position where it is difficult to use.

The shoulder lift is the most valuable tool you can teach your defensive linemen. This technique is the best method your defensive linemen have to meet an offensive lineman head-on. If a lineman cannot neutralize an offensive charge with the shoulder lift, he is not going to help your defensive line.

The main physical trait needed for the shoulder lift is leg strength, which should be common to all your linemen. The technique is well suited to your short stocky linemen. The lack of height is advantageous to helping them get under the offensive linemen and work up through them. Naturally, the taller player with the strong shoulder, forearm, and upper body can use this technique as well as any of the others.

The shoulder lift is most effectively used when you want your lineman to play head-up and control the gap on either side

If you want your lineman to control a gap on one side or the other, the shoulder lift can be executed on the respective side of the offensive man whom you want to control. When the lift is performed on the side, the opposite hand is used to push upward on the opponent's shoulder pads, on the outside of his arm, just below his shoulder.

To summarize, all your defensive linemen must master the shoulder lift. You can most effectively use it to control a man head-up. You can also use it to control a shoulder or gap. The points you should emphasize in teaching the shoulder lift are:

1. The tail must be slightly lower than the shoulders to insure the inclined angle of the back.

2. The blow must be delivered on the front of the opponent's pads, just above the numbers.

3. The thrust must be on the angle of an inclined plane.

When your defensive linemen successfully execute the shoulder lift, they will neutralize the charge of the offensive man and be in a position to carry out the defensive responsibilities.

2. Forearm Lift

Another technique common to the defensive lineman is the forearm lift. Mastering this charge in addition to the shoulder lift gives the defender an additional method of controlling the offensive lineman. Common denominators among most of the techniques facilitate teaching them.

The forearm lift is executed by quickly bringing up the top of the forearm, keeping it parallel to the ground, and striking it on the front part of the opponent's pads, just above the numbers. (See Figure 2-2.) Contact is made at the same point that it is made with the shoulder lift. The opposite hand pushes back on the shoulder on the opposite side. This is also similar to the shoulder lift.

Getting off the ball and attacking from the bottom up cannot be overemphasized. The tail must be lower than the shoulders and the back at a slight angle. The thrust behind the blow comes from the legs. The leg technique is similar to that of the shoulder lift.

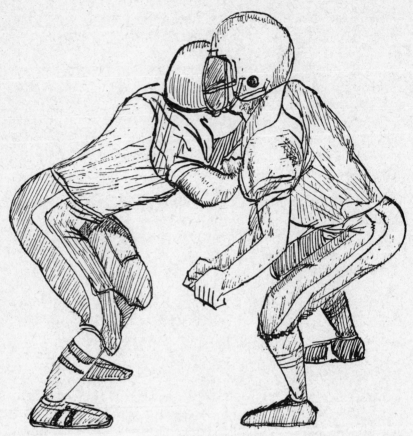

Figure 2-2

The physical characteristic needed to execute a good forearm lift is a strong forearm. This charge requires more arm strength than the shoulder lift. Since the forearm absorbs the brunt of the blow, a forearm pad is recommended. A pad will not only cushion the impact of the forearm charge, but will also cushion some of the other charges as well. A soft shock absorber will also curtail any hesitation a lineman may have about bruising his arm on his opponent's equipment.

Some of your linemen will not have the arm strength to execute the forearm lift. This technique is not as critical to your defensive line play as the shoulder lift, but it can be a valuable asset to your linemen who have the arm strength.

The forearm lift allows your linemen to neutralize and control a man—keeping a distance between the defender and his man. The extended arm protects the midsection of the defender.

3. Vertical Elbow Lift

In addition to the shoulder lift and the forearm lift, another valuable charge for defensive linemen is the vertical elbow lift. The vertical elbow can easily be used as a defender's primary charge. This technique has much in common with the shoulder lift and the forearm lift.

The vertical lift is executed by delivering a blow with the bent elbow in a vertical position. (See Figure 2-3.) The elbow

Figure 2-3

and arm make contact at the front of the opponent's pads, just above the numbers. The wrist and hand go into the "V" of the man's neck and shoulder. The blow is delivered in the same location as that of the shoulder lift and forearm lift. The heel of the opposite hand is placed under the shoulder pad, similar to the other two charges.

The directional force of the elbow lift is determined by the defender's responsibility. If the defender's responsibility is to control a shoulder or inside gap, the pressure of the elbow is directed up and through the side of the neck. The opposite hand force is applied across the same direction.

If the defender's responsibility is to play head-up and control the gap on either side, the force is applied up and straight back. The thrust of the blow comes mainly from the on-side leg, similar to the previously mentioned charges. The opposite leg is also the same.

In the execution of all charges, the head establishes the angle that the remainder of the body will follow. The chin is tucked to keep the angle of the blow from going straight up. The blow should follow the same path as that of the shoulder lift and forearm lift.

Your linemen can most effectively use this technique when you want them to control a shoulder or inside gap because most of the initial force is directed to one side of the offensive man. When you want your linemen to use it to control one side, you must emphasize the force applied through the neck to force the man to the opposite side. When you want your defender to control both sides, emphasize the force directed straight back and up.

The vertical lift technique requires some additional development by your linemen if they use their opposite arms. If you do not develop their opposite sides, they are likely to execute the blow with less abandon than they would their stronger arms. You must be careful not to weaken a defense by placing a lineman in a position where he is constantly using his weaker side. If you have a lineman who is right-handed and playing a shoulder or gap on the right defensive side, he is constantly making contact with his weaker side. Your practice time should allow him to develop his weaker side. This applies not only to the striking part of the body, but also to the opposite thrusting leg. You do not have to spend as much time developing an opposite shoulder as you do an opposite forearm or elbow.

After you have taught the shoulder lift and the forearm lift, the vertical elbow lift will be easy to teach because of all that it has in common with the other two charges. All three techniques have the same:

1. Location of blow
2. Angle of thrust
3. Leg push
4. Position of opposite hand

The vertical elbow lift is another method that your defensive linemen have to win the most critical collision in football—the one-on-one.

4. Two-Handed Shoulder Shiver

The two-handed shoulder shiver is an additional defensive charge which the defensive linemen may use. Utilized with the other techniques, it is an effective weapon.

The two-handed shoulder shiver is executed by quickly bringing up the heels of both hands and striking a sharp blow under each shoulder of the óffensive man. (See Figure 2-4). At the moment of contact, the elbows are locked rigid. The idea of attacking from the bottom up cannot be overemphasized. The angle of the force is critical if the defender is to control his man.

A quick start off the ball is more imperative to the shoulder shiver than to some of the other initial charges. It is important because the hands and extended arms are all that protect the defender's body from the offensive charge. The defender must get his elbows locked as soon as possible. If they are not locked, he cannot possibly hold off the offensive man's entire body weight.

Your linemen can best use the shoulder shiver to control a man head-up. They will not be as aggressive with the shiver as they'll be with the shoulder lift, forearm lift, or vertical elbow

Figure 2-4

lift, but the limited contact with the offensive man allows your linemen to quickly get to the ball. You can easily adapt the shiver to reading-type defenses. The extended arms keep the opponent away while your linemen can read and react. The extension also allows your linemen time to read and react to long yardage situations such as screens, draws, passes, and outside plays.

The shoulder shiver is a good charge for your linemen to use in situations when the offense is likely to run a play other than something that hits quickly. We would not recommend your linemen using this technique when the play is likely to be hitting quickly or directly unless they have excellent arm strength.

Every defensive charge is not for all of your defensive linemen. The shiver is especially difficult for your linemen who lack the arm strength. However, the more techniques your linemen

can master, the better you will have them prepared to successfully carry out their assignments.

5. Goal Line Charge

The goal line charge is one of the most critical charges in
football. The proper execution of this charge can prevent a score
or stop a critical short yardage play. The technique should not be
overlooked as a method of penetrating into the opponent's
backfield. It can also be used to beat the two-on-one.

The proper execution of the goal line charge begins with the
proper stance (Figure 2-5), which varies widely from the stance
of other charges. The objective of the goal line charge is to get
one yard into the backfield. The pursuit necessary for other
situations is secondary on the goal line. The first responsibility of
the goal line charge is to stop the direct play—with no gain. The
stance used for the goal line charge is designed to get the defender into the backfield and stop the back before he can get
started.

Figure 2-5

The hands are placed on the ground, slightly in front of the shoulders. The fingers, spread as far as possible, make direct contact with the ground. They are spread and low so that the defensive man can push off them when the offensive man moves. The shoulders, almost directly above the hands, are parallel to the ground and approximately six inches above it. The elbows are bent at right angles. The head is extremely low and tilted back. It must be up on the ball as far as possible, making sure that the helmet does not break the plane of the neutral zone. The tail is high so that the head and shoulders can get low. The legs are under the tail so that the body weight is forward.

The eyes are directed at the hands of the nearest offensive lineman; at the first instance that the hands move forward, the defensive linemen must simultaneously push off their hands and feet. The key to winning the one-on-one on the goal line is keeping the shoulders low when coming off the ball. Whoever keeps his shoulders lower will win the one-on-one.

The goal line charge will vary according to the defensive responsibility that you give your linemen. If you want them to play a shoulder, have them make shoulder contact on the opponent's thigh. Aiming for the thigh will keep your linemen low. After contact is made, your linemen must be squared up and perpendicular to the line of scrimmage. From this position, the elbows and arms are extended so that they are like hooks on either side of the shoulders. You now have your lineman ready to attack any back that comes near him. His tackle must be sure; stopping the progress of the ball is more important than stopping the progress of the back.

Your linemen will use another variation of the goal line charge when you want them to control a gap. You must first have them penetrate into the gap to a point one yard into the backfield. Do not let them overpenetrate as that will position them out of the play. To have your linemen get through the smaller gap caused by the tightening of the offensive line, have them turn their shoulders from parallel to the ground, to perpendicular to the ground. The shoulders are turned as soon as they get into the neutral zone. The twisting of the shoulders reduces their shoulder surface, enabling them to get through a limited opening. They no longer need a clearance area equal to the width of their shoulder pads. As soon as the gap is cleared, they return to the parallel position and defend their ground as described earlier.

To summarize, no charge is more important to your defensive linemen than the goal line charge. Their failure to execute any part of the technique may result in a score. The coaching points of the goal line charge are as follows:

1. The shoulders must be extremely low to the ground so that contact is made under the shoulders of the offensive man.

2. The shoulders must be twisted to get through a gap.

3. The defended area must not be overpenetrated.

4. Once in the gap, the attacking area of the defender must be extended as wide as possible.

5. Stopping the progress of the ball is more important than stopping the progress of the back.

6. Over the Top

The over-the-top technique is not used very often, but knowing the technique will have your linemen prepared to take advantage of an opportunity to use it. The charge is used infrequently, but it may put your linemen in position to make the big play in your opponent's backfield. It's a big play technique that can often change the momentum of a game. You can often trace momentum to someone doing something little but effectively—like using a seldom-used technique at the correct time.

The over-the-top technique is executed by literally going over the top of the offensive man. Obviously, this cannot be done at will by the defender. You must teach your linemen to recognize certain faults in the charge of the offensive lineman. The one major flaw that they should look for is too low a charge. This happens to an offensive lineman when his head is too low. Sometimes the fault is indicated by the stance of the offensive lineman. If he aligns with his tail up and his head down, the back will be on an angle aimed at the ground. This kind of poor stance is frequent when a lineman is tired.

When the offensive man comes off the ball low, the defender has an excellent opportunity to use the over-the-top charge.

He does it by pushing down sharply on the back of the opponent's pads. He pushes him down in the direction that he is already headed—to the ground. As he pushes his man down, he straddles over his man's body. This will quickly put the defensive man into the backfield.

This technique is adaptive to your small, quick linemen. More important than quickness, your linemen must be intelligent to recognize the flaw in the offensive lineman. Over-the-top is a good technique for your linemen to know, and it can often lead to a defensive game-breaker.

7. Submarine

You can put the submarine charge in the same category as the over-the-top technique. Your linemen will not use it very often, but when they do use it, it can change the momentum of a game. The submarine, when used with over-the-top and the lifts and shivers, can very effectively challenge any offensive lineman.

The submarine is executed by coming off the ball on all fours, hands and feet, and scrambling through the legs or on the side of the offensive man. Naturally, it is most effectively used by your smaller, quicker lineman. Similar to over-the-top, the properly executed submarine puts the defensive man quickly into the backfield where he is in position to make the big play.

The submarine has an effective variation when the defender has a gap responsibility. By aligning away from the assigned area as we discussed in Chapter 1, the quick defender can submarine to the right or left of his man and get to his assigned area.

Your linemen should use the submarine and over-the-top charges when penetration is necessary. Your players need more quickness than strength to properly execute these techniques. They are techniques that are not used very often, but when they are used, they make something happen.

Winning the Stalemate

The first step for your linemen to win the one-on-one, the most critical collision in football, is to get off the ball on movement with a good charge technique. If your defender and the opponent are of equal or near equal ability, they will come to a neutral position—the stalemate. The stalemate is the time during the one-on-one when the force of the offensive man is equal to the force of the defensive man.

The key to your linemen winning the one-on-one, specifically the stalemate, is their being the first to recover motion after the stalemate is reached. The recovery movement begins with the feet. Since the thrust of the charge comes from the feet, they must be planted firmly at the moment of contact. They must start to move again immediately after contact is made. Whoever moves his feet more quickly will momentarily be pushing a stationary object. This is where we get the idea that getting the jump is worth fifty pounds.

If your lineman can quickly get to his man or meet him half-way in the neutral zone, neutralize him, and be the first to recover from the stalemate, he will be working against a stationary object and be in excellent position to execute his responsibilities.

Applying the Principle of the Inclined Plane

After your linemen neutralize the offensive charge with a good technique and react first to the stalemate, they are faced with the problem of controlling the force of the offensive man. They can control that force by applying a simple technique of physics—the inclined plane.

The inclined plane gives your linemen the easiest way to lift and control a heavier force or object. It allows your linemen to gradually push back the force of the offensive charge.

If your linemen are to successfully control their opponents by applying the principle of the inclined plane, they must do the following:

1. Deliver a blow with their tails lower than their shoulders.
2. Make contact under the shoulders of their man.
3. Direct the force of the blow on an upward angle, similar to a shark leaping out of the water.

Equalizing Uneven Match-Ups

Frequently, one of your defensive linemen will match up, one-on-one, with an exceptional offensive lineman who is physically and technically superior to your defender. The worst thing that you can do is to ask your lineman to play him head-up and control each side of him.

You must make adjustments so that your lineman and your defense are not at a disadvantage. Adjustments that you may make to equalize an uneven match-up include the following:

1. Neutralize the superior offensive player by playing your best defensive player head-up on him—provided your lineman has near equal ability.

2. Play your defense so that you have a man playing on his weaker shoulder—preferably with your man using his stronger shoulder.

3. Play your quickest man head-up and use a defense that allows your man to penetrate the gap on either side of the superior man. Be sure to have a linebacker cover the gap that he doesn't penetrate.

4. Play your defense unbalanced to the side of the superior man.

5. Play a stack on the superior lineman so that a linebacker can read the superior man's block.

The method that you choose to try to equalize the uneven match-up depends on the material that you have available and the defense that you use. In most cases you cannot change your material, so you must change your defense.

In conclusion, the defensive charges that you choose to teach are dictated by:

1. The type of defense you use
2. The responsibilities your linemen have
3. The physical limitations of each player

Some of the techniques are primary charges that are common to all defensive line play. They include:

1. The shoulder lift
2. The forearm lift
3. The vertical elbow lift
4. The goal line charge

The other charges are most effectively used in special situations. These secondary techniques are frequently game-breakers.

A good defensive charge, which follows a good stance and quick start, will put your defender into a stalemate position with his man. To win the stalemate, he must be the first to recover from neutralization and apply force on an upward angle—like a shark leaping out of the water. The offensive man can easily be controlled if the force is applied on the angle of an inclined plane.

Football reduced to its simplest terms is the one-on-one. The more collisions you win, the better your team's chance of winning. You can increase your team's chances of winning more one-on-one's by:

1. Perfecting initial charges
2. Teaching charges commensurate with your player's ability and his assignment
3. Equalizing match-ups

After you teach your linemen the basics of winning the one-on-one, you are ready to give them the specifics of defending the area from tackle to tackle.

DRILLS

1. Sadie Hawkins Day.

Purpose: To develop weaker side charges.

Procedure: One practice period per week is designated as Sadie Hawkins Day. All players execute skills and drills with their opposite side.

Comment: Particular attention should be devoted to developing forearms and shoulders that will be regularly used. Some players are extremely weak with their opposite side.

2. Off Your Mark.

Purpose: To develop quickness by having players make contact on the offensive side or in the neutral zone.

Procedure: Set up one-on-one. Be sure players are separated a ball's width; the distance should be farther if stunting defenses are used. Make a mark behind the heels of the defensive player. He moves when the hands of the offensive player move. He must make contact "off his mark."

Comment: Demand that contact be made on the offensive side, but accept it being made in the neutral zone.

3. One-on-One.

Purpose: To develop movement on movement. To make contact in the neutral zone. To develop charge techniques.

Procedure: Set up one-on-one. Players execute defensive charges.

Comment: Emphasis should be on primary charges. In all drills, be sure to give more positive remarks than negative remarks.

4. The Rating Game.

Purpose: To develop form of charges.

Procedure: Each defender has a man on whom he executes the final position of the initial charges. Each player displays his form as you rate him from one to ten.

Comment: In addition to developing pride in the technique, players will develop a "feel" for the final position of each charge.

5. Recline Bag Drill.

Purpose: To develop hitting angle for initial charges.

Procedure: Two players hold a bag on an inclined angle. Defender executes his charge by hitting up through the bag.

Comment: To make the drill a strength exercise, have the holders apply resistance as contact is made. If the defender's back is not on the proper angle, he will have difficulty delivering force through the bag.

3

Coaching the Defensive Area from Tackle to Tackle

Aggressive even-man play. Making your nose guard a nuisance. Defensing the off-tackle. Reading men in the area. Defeating the double team.

The effectiveness of your run defense is determined by how well you defend the area from tackle to tackle. This is the first line of our strength up the middle. Initial control of this area is important because most opponents try to establish a running game before they look for a passing game. How well you control that running game is directly related to the skills and techniques of your inside linemen.

Chapter 2 explained the first major step in defending that area, winning the one-on-one; but, in addition to winning individual battles, each inside position has different skills and responsibilities that must be performed. The better their jobs are carried out, the better your inside linemen will defend the run.

Aggressive Even-Man Play

You may call your inside men guards or you may call them tackles, but whatever you call them, you'd better call them aggressive.

The skills that make your inside men aggressive are dictated by the types of plays common to the middle area:

1. Quick-hitting (dives, powers, sneaks)
2. Delays (traps, counters, draws, reverses)

To defend against this variety of plays, your defensive guards must be intelligent as well as skilled.

The guards must be intelligent to recognize the specific keys that are given for plays that are common to the area they are defending. Once they recognize a particular play, they must have the skill to stop it.

One type of alignment to stop these plays is the even-man look. This type of defense gives you two linemen to defend the offensive area from guard to guard.

An initial maneuver for these two men is to vary their alignment so that their offensive counterparts do not get a sense of security about the defensive look. When the guards change looks, one of them should take the responsibility of remaining close to the center to cover the quick sneak. We like to give this responsibility to our right guard because without our right guard, we're defenseless.

Regardless of where they line up, you should expect both guards to get one yard into the offensive backfield. Realistically, you should be satisfied if the players can consistently maintain a stalemate at the line of scrimmage. A stalemate at the line will defend quick-hitting plays because it will prevent any openings in the offensive line and it will keep the offensive linemen from attacking your linebackers (or linebacker).

Occasionally, interior linemen will become overaggressive and get deeper than one yard into the backfield. When they overpenetrate in this way, they become vulnerable to the trap and they create "air pockets" in the defense by giving the defenders on each side more area to cover. (See Figure 3-1.)

Figure 3-1

The guards must avoid causing an "air pocket" and do everything they can to prevent any openings in the offensive line. They prevent openings by being as much of an obstacle as possible. Guards offer the least resistance when they are flat on the ground. From the prone position, the only opportunity a defensive linemen has to make a tackle is to make a lucky reach or, even more fortunately, have the back trip over him.

The least that is expected from any defensive lineman is a position of all fours (hands and feet) with the tail up in the air. This is the minimum expected to protect an area, particularly the inside area.

Guard responsibilities include pursuit on inside and outside plays. The technique to pursue an inside play is to shed the blocker and take a direct path to the ball carrier. During any pursuit from tackle to tackle, the shoulders should be kept parallel to the line of scrimmage and the body should be squared up. This hitting position will allow the guards to deliver a blow if they meet resistance on the way to the ball carrier. If the ball

Figure 3-2

carrier is outside the tackles and there is no threat of a reverse coming back inside, the guards should take an angle of pursuit to be where the back will be. (See Figure 3-2.)

When your inside linemen are stopping the plays directly at them and they are pursuing the ball inside and outside, they are making a valuable contribution to your defense. Their aggressiveness will be evident.

Making Your Nose Guard a Nuisance

The other type of middle play is the odd alignment, and successful odd-man alignments are predicated on a good nose man. If you compare nose-guard play to even-guard play, the former must do the job that both guards do in even defenses. This puts a lot of pressure on the nose guard.

Since the play of the point man is so crucial, you should not be thinking of playing odd defenses unless you first have a nose man who is good enough to make the defense go. Currently there are no shortages of good nose guards, as evidenced by the popularity of the 52 defense, or, a lot of coaches are in the wrong defense.

The 52 and the odd-man variations from it give a lot of responsibility to the middle man. His major run responsibilities are:

1. Defending tackle to tackle
2. Pursuing to the outside
3. Rushing the passer from the inside
4. Stopping the middle draw

To successfully carry out these duties, he must be familiar with a myriad of techniques. At the beginning of every play he must use a one-on-one technique that neutralizes the block of the center. If he has a head-up responsibility, he can use any of the initial charges that allow him to control the gaps on either side. If he slants to either side, he can use any of the shoulder techniques that give him a free arm and leg with which to control his gap. All these techniques, gaps and head-up, are described in Chapter 2.

If your nose guard plays a soft type of technique, he can more effectively use some other techniques that are more esoteric to his position. The philosophy of soft nose-guard play is to get maximum pursuit from tackle to tackle while sacrificing some aggressiveness on direct hits up the middle. A combination of the two types of philosophies can be a problem for the offense.

The soft philosophy is a hit-and-run technique. The idea is for the nose guard to check the middle by making aggressive contact with the center and then pursue to the side of the play.

Another soft type of technique is to key the direction of the play by reading the head of the center. If your scouting report shows that the center will take the nose guard one-on-one, you can use the center's block as a directional key for the play. The technique for reading this type of block is to cross-face the center in the direction of the play.

The cross-face technique is executed by getting the bicep of the arm across the helmet of the blocker and into the gap that the blocker is trying to clear. If your nose guard has difficulty reading the direction of the play, he can back off the ball to get a longer read. As a general rule, the more experienced your nose guard, the closer he can be on the ball to read his key.

An additional keying type of technique for the nose guard is to hit the center and read the feet of the quarterback. If your scouting report shows that your opponent's quarterback doesn't use a reverse pivot, you have a fairly reliable key for your nose man to read the direction of the play.

The nose guard reads the quarterback's feet by first hitting the center with a head-up technique, preferably a two-handed shoulder shiver, and then reacting to the side of the quarterback's first open step. The middle man's technique is to roll the back of the shoulder to the side of the read. This is best done by shooting the arm underneath to the side of the read.

A more aggressive type of nose-guard play is to read the downblocks of the offensive guards. If you are running an effective 52, the on-side offensive guard should have to help the center with the block on the nose guard. If your nose guard can be consistently handled one-on-one by the center, you should consider some other defenses, or you'd better have some super linebackers.

Assuming that one offensive guard will consistently be coming down on the nose guard, you can use this angle block for a directional key. The nose guard reads the angle block by rolling to the side from which he is getting the pressure, the side of the angle block. (See Figure 3-3.)

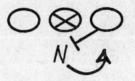

Figure 3-3

This technique, as well as the others mentioned, will give you heavy inside pursuit by your nose guard. The keying techniques will get him there in enough time to get his nose into the play.

In addition to pursuing on inside plays, many nose guards can utilize their quickness by pursuing outside plays as well. Many good nose men can cover the field by pursuing from sideline to sideline. The key to a nose guard having this range is his getting a good angle of pursuit after he clears the tackle. He must patrol the tackle areas with a squared-up position, but as

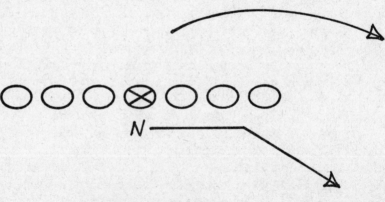

Figure 3-4

soon as he clears the tackle he must take a good deep angle to
the ball carrier. (See Figure 3-4.) Details of pursuing are discussed in Chapter 7.

Defending the Off Tackle

Defensive strength up the middle is important, but you
cannot have a strong defense unless you have strong tackles. The
old coaches, the ones who danced to the Box Shift, say, "So go
the tackles, so goes the defense."

You don't realize the importance of tackles to a good defense until you try to develop a defense without good tackles.
The location of their position gives them the following run responsibilities:

1. Pursuing inside
2. Pursuing outside
3. Stopping the off-tackle

The most difficult assignment of the three is stopping the
off-tackle play. To do this, they must be able to maintain a
stalemate at the point of attack. A tackle has the added problem
of being down-blocked by the tight end. In essence, he must
have the strength to go one-on-one against the offensive tackle
and the agility to react to the pressure of an angle block.

In addition to defending the off-tackle play, the off-tackle
defender plays a major role on inside pursuit and outside pursuit. When he clearly sees the ball cross the line of scrimmage
he must take a direct path to be in front of the ball carrier. (See
Figure 3-5.)

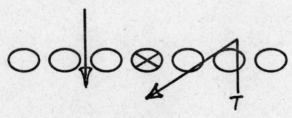

Figure 3-5

Outside pursuit can be made with less caution. A tackle has more keys for recognizing an outside play than for an inside play. The following keys are helpful for recognizing outside plays:

1. A guard or guards pulling with depth
2. A tackle pulling
3. A wingback blocking down
4. A back running outside, parallel to the line or running away from the line (quick pitch)

The most obvious key for recognizing an outside play is seeing the ball go outside. When the ball goes out, the player should go out. If he leaves before the ball goes out, he is vulnerable to being trapped.

Reading Men in the Area

A defensive lineman's surest key for locating the ball is to read the blocking pattern of the offensive men in his area. The traditional technique is for the defensive linemen to read the offensive linemen as if it were a three-on-one drill. The defender should read and react accordingly:

1. If he is blocked by the man directly in front of him, he must fight the direct pressure and strive to keep the hole as impassable as possible. As mentioned previously, the least expected of defensive linemen is to clog the hole by staying on all fours.
2. If he is blocked by the opponent on either side of him, he must roll to the side of the pressure. (See Figure 3-6.)

Figure 3-6

3. If the man directly on him pulls in either direction, the defensive lineman should mirror the pull (Figure 3-7), staying on the defensive side of the line of scrimmage. This mirroring of the pulling guard must be done with caution if the opponent has shown a sucker trap play where the offense runs a back naked into the hole of the pulling lineman. (See Figure 3-8.) The sucker trap play is more the exception than the rule.

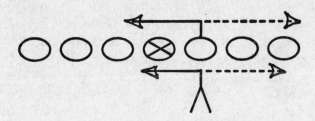

Figure 3-7

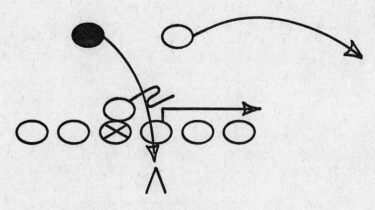

Figure 3-8

4. If the defensive lineman is not blocked, he should look inside, expecting to meet the trap man. If the defensive man is neither trapped nor blocked, he's not near the play.

5. If the opponent retreats to pass block, the defender should think draw and screen and use a pass rush technique.

6. If the opponent releases to either side, the defender

should give him a shoulder shiver to knock him off balance and prevent him from blocking the defensive man on either side.

Reading the inside release has become more significant with the option offenses. The defensive lineman has the difficult problem of distinguishing between the traditional inside release to block downfield and the currently popular reach block to screen a defensive lineman from a quick-hitting dive.

A key to distinguishing between the reach and the release is reading the height of the offensive man's helmet. If his helmet is high, the offensive man is releasing to go downfield. If his helmet is low, he is attempting to reach block or hook.

After your defensive lineman correctly recognizes the reach block or hook, he must react to it. The reacting must be quick because the plays behind these types of blocks are quick-hitting.

The reaction technique to the reach block is the cross-face technique. This technique is commonly used by the nose guard. It is executed by shooting the upper arm and back of the shoulder through the head of the blocker, getting inside position in the gap that the offensive man is trying to screen. As soon as the defender gets a shoulder past the offensive man's helmet, the defensive man is in position to make the tackle.

Defeating the Double Team

Another offensive maneuver, easier to read but harder to react to, is the double team. The double team is a reliable key to where the play is being run. Only an unusual offensive pattern would use a double team away from the point of attack.

Defending the double team and reacting to it are much more difficult than seeing it. We defend double teams with a minimum requirement philosophy. Our linemen know that the least expected from them when they are double teamed is to maintain the ground where they started the play. If they can do more than this, we are elated. If they do less, we have a problem.

There are three common defensive techniques for beating or neutralizing the double team:

1. Maintaining the area on all fours
2. Knifing the shoulders through the two offensive men (See Figure 3-9.)
3. Rolling to the side of the pressure

Figure 3-9

The double team area can be successfully defended if the defensive man can hold his ground because he will keep the hole closed that the offense is trying to open. The two men trying to open the hole will actually be defending it when they can not get the defensive man out of the hole.

The hole can be kept closed by the defensive man going to an all four position when he recognizes the second blocker trying to move him. The key to not being driven back and the theme of Chapter 2 is to come off the ball low. If the shoulders are low, neither blocker will be in a position to drive back the defensive man. As soon as the defensive man's shoulders come up, an offensive man will drive him back and two offensive men will drive him back twice as far.

Another technique for defending the double team is to roll off the side of the downblock pressure. In most double team situations, the defensive man will be hitting his man head-up, and he will be doubled down by an offensive man on either side. When the pressure is felt from the side, the defensive man can roll into the side of the play. The pressure side will always be the side of the ball carrier. The coaching points of the rolls are discussed in Chapter 7.

The third double team defensive technique is best used when the defensive man expects the double team, or he is assigned to play a gap where he can easily be blocked by both offensive men. The knifing technique is executed by the defender, turning his shoulders from parallel to the ground to perpendicular to the ground and knifing the shoulders through the two offensive men. Once the defensive man has his shoulders in back of the offensive men, a successful block cannot be executed.

In conclusion, aggressive linemen make an aggressive defense. You can make your interior linemen aggressive by teaching them their responsibilities and then teaching them how to react to the offensive linemen who are attempting to prevent the defense from carrying out their assignment.

Specifically, defensive linemen must know how to react to running plays peculiar to their defensive area. Generally, they must know how to read the blocking patterns of the offensive men near them. Teaching defensive linemen to react to blocking patterns will assure you that your interior linemen will be where the ball is. Chapter 4 will help you get your defensive ends there also.

DRILLS

1. Reading Drills.

Purpose: To teach reading offensive men in area.

Procedure: Three offensive men face one defensive man. The offensive men use various offensive patterns: head on, pulls, slants, double team, pass block.

Comment: The reactions of the three-on-one drill can be reduced to one-on-one or two-on-one, or they can be extended to five-on-two or a full-line scrimmage.

2. Nose Guard Keys.

Purpose: To teach the nose guard to read directional keys.

Procedure: Nose guard goes one-on-one with center. Nose guard goes one-on-one with the center and a quarterback behind the center. Nose guard reads directional key from the center and/or quarterbacks.

Comment: This specialized one-on-one drill is used to develop whatever keys you use for your nose man.

3. Tackle Read and Pursuit.

Purpose: To teach tackles to react to their keys and pursue the ball.

Procedure: Tackle lines up where he would normally be in one of your defenses. He then reacts to his various keys and pursues the football inside or outside.

Comment: Similar to the nose guard drill, this drill is used to develop whatever keys you use in your defense. In addition to line keys, you can also use back keys and ball keys.

4. Team Pursuit Drill.

Purpose: To make every defensive lineman aware that he has a definite responsibility and place to be on every play. To encourage team pursuit. To encourage gang tackling. To encourage second-line tacklers to go for the ball.

Procedure: Set up a defensive line against an offense. Give the offense three basic plays to run: one inside and one outside to both sides. The defensive linemen react to each play. Figure 3-10 shows the defensive reaction to an inside play. Figure 3-11 shows their reaction to an outside play.

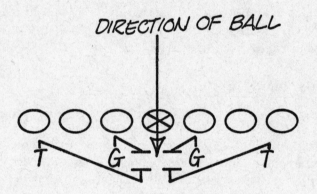

Figure 3-10

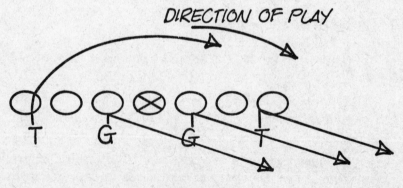

Figure 3-11

Comment: Before you start the drill, walk each player through his angle of pursuit and final position when the ball goes inside and outside to either side. Emphasize speed getting to the ball, but make sure initial responsibilities are covered. Occasionally, run a bootleg or change-up play to insure covering of basic responsibilities.

4

Developing
the Defensive End

*Standing up vs 3-point stance.   Crashing.   Pursuing out-
side plays.   Preventing the bootleg.   Pursuing inside
plays.   Playing pass responsibilities.*

The first priority in designing a defense is to take away the
bomb. The second most critical area to defend is the perimeter.
Protection of the perimeter is determined by the type of play
you get from your outside defensive linemen—your defensive
ends. Coaching philosophies of end play may vary, but certain
techniques are common to all types of end play.

The type of stance you choose for your defensive end should
be determined by assignment and responsibility. Each kind of
stance has its advantages and disadvantages.

The two point stance is advantageous to an end that crashes.
When you crash your end, he should upset the offensive pattern
as much as possible—even if the play goes in the opposite direction. Crashing an end is more than a hit or miss play. It should
force the opponent to make some change in their offensive pattern.

Whether your ends crash or contain, you must get as much pursuit as possible from them because you don't have any pursuing linemen outside them. Since ends are basically linemen, pass responsibility is a unique experience for them. Teaching them to cover a pass can be very challenging for you.

Standing Up vs 3-Point Stance

The stance of your defensive end should be determined by his responsibilities and since responsibilities change from situation to situation, it is feasible that the end's stance will change from situation to situation. Naturally, the 3-point stance is stronger against the run because the end is more difficult to block in a down position than in an up position.

Figure 4-1

In the up position (see Figure 4-1), the end has better vision and can better see the play develop. From the up position, he can better react laterally since he doesn't have as much weight forward.

In Pro defenses, the defensive end (the last lineman on the end of the line) has primarily run responsibility and usually no pass drop responsibility so his natural stance would be down. But if he is located on the split-end side where there is no danger of a tight end blocking down on him, there is some value in aligning him in an up position. The up position in this situation would give him the following advantages:

1. Better vision of the development of the play

2. Position where the quarterback would have to throw through the end to hit the split receiver on short slant patterns (see Figure 4-2)

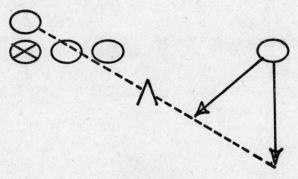

Figure 4-2

3. Quick access to pursue outside plays such as quick pitches and sweeps

If your opponent has a tendency to run off tackle to the split side or if your split side lineman has dive responsibility on the option, he should always be down.

The two-point stance is the most effective stance in defenses where the end has outside contain responsibility. The up-stance better allows the defensive end to perform his basic responsibilities, which are:

1. Avoid being hooked.
2. Close down the off-tackle hole.
3. Delay the end on pass patterns.
4. Obstruct the end from closing down on the tackle or linebacker.
5. Play pass responsibility, either rush or drop.

A defensive end lines up in a two-point stance by placing his inside foot up and his outside foot back. The palms of both hands should extend in front of the inside leg. The height of the hands should be just above the knee.

The extended hands and the inside knee are the first two lines of defense that protect the body. Both lines of defense make your end safe from what both of you should fear—the end being hooked. The usual alignment of the two-point stance is on the outside shoulder of the end man on the offensive line. That offensive person could be a tight end, tackle, or wingback.

From the outside alignment, the defensive end should take his first step with his inside foot. With the first step, the hands should make solid contact with the offensive man. This contact will prevent the opponent from coming off the line quickly and making a down block or running a quick pass pattern.

Crashing

An effective method to pressure the corners is to crash the ends. Crashing ends force offenses and can effectively reduce the options of an option offense. An option quarterback facing a crashing end has only one option—to give the ball to someone else.

Whether the play is an option or something other, the crashing end must get into the backfield as quickly as possible and be as destructive as possible. To get into the backfield as quickly as possible, the end should align in a straight line with the outside shoulder of the offensive end and the outside thigh of the nearest back (see Figure 4-3). He should line up tight on the line of scrimmage so that he reduces the distance to the offensive backfield. On the first movement of the offensive end, the defensive end should go through the shoulder of the offensive end and aim directly for the outside thigh of his key back. If the play is a run, the end should knock down everyone who comes near him. If he doesn't make the tackle, he should eliminate the interference in front of the ball carrier.

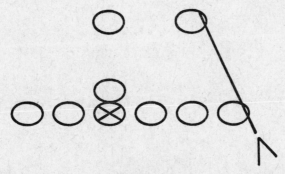

Figure 4-3

If the play is a pass when he crashes, he should pressure the passer, but he can also cause other problems along the way. If he makes contact with the back who is blocking for the passer, he will help defend against the screen and draw.

Contact with the draw back will upset the exchange timing between the draw back and the quarterback. Also, the timing for a screen will be upset if the blocking back is headed for a screen pass in the flat. In both situations, the crashing end would upset the timing of the play.

If the play goes in the opposite direction of the crashing end for a roll-out pass or a run, the defensive end is not totally ineffective. Backside pressure (Figure 4-4) will not always stop a play, but it may cause the play to develop more quickly than normal and once again upset the timing of the play. Also, a crashing end, pursuing from the backside, will be in excellent position to stop the reverse.

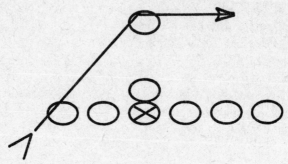

Figure 4-4

Pursuing Outside Plays

When an end is not crashing, he is usually either playing a contain end or a force end. When your end has either of these responsibilities, it is imperative that he line up in a stance that eliminates his being hooked. This is the first step in pursuing outside plays—avoid being hooked.

If your defense dictates a contain end, your end must get to the outside on the first indication of an outside play. Your defensive end can anticipate an outside play by reacting to the following keys:

1. A guard or tackle pulling to the outside
2. A back going outside
3. The ball going outside

Once the outside key is recognized, some inexperienced contain ends make the mistake of playing the contain from too far outside. If your end is too wide, the ball carrier can run inside him and still get outside the defense (see Figure 4-5). When your end is playing outside contain, he must hold the corner so that the force part of the defense can force the ball carrier into the containing end.

The outside pursuit of a forcing end is not as critical as a containing end, but it is important. A forcing end is slower to react to the outside than a containing end because the forcing

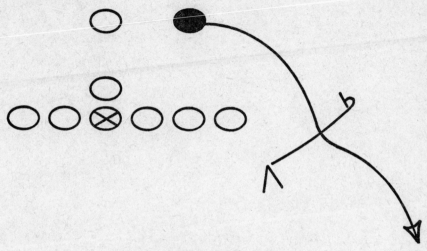

Figure 4-5

end will have responsibility off-tackle. A good rule for a forcing
end to pursue outside is: "Ball goes, I go." The angle of pursuit
for an outside play is the most important angle in football. If the
angle is too short, the offense is sure to make the big play. The
depth of the angle is determined by three factors:

1. The speed of the defensive end
2. The speed of the ball carrier
3. The proximity of the sideline

The slower the end, the deeper the angle. The faster the
ball carrier, the deeper the angle. The farther away the sideline,
the deeper the angle. The average depth for an average end is
about two yards deep on the defensive side of the line of scrimmage (see Figure 4-6). You will find teaching this angle is difficult because it is unnatural for a defender to run away from the
ball carrier and then have the ball carrier catch up to him.

The outside pursuit technique is similar to the method of
pursuing a roll-out quarterback. When an improper technique is
used against the roll-out, the corner becomes extremely vulnerable. The difficulty of defending the roll-out, similar to pursuing

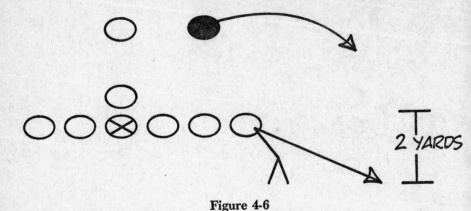

Figure 4-6

the outside, is that the defensive end must unnaturally run away from the direction of the quarterback.

When the defensive end reads that the quarterback is rolling out, he must use a flattening-out technique that will take him to his outside angle of pursuit. This technique will put the defensive end in position to execute his responsibilities, whether they be pressure or pass drop.

Preventing the Bootleg

Another important outside responsibility of a defensive end is to protect against the bootleg. This play can be a game-breaker if not properly defended. In every type of defense, someone has to be responsible for the bootleg. Usually, it is the job of the defensive end. The end must be conditioned to think bootleg every time the play goes away from him. The offense usually calls this play after carefully observing backside reaction when the play goes wide. The offense will call the bootleg when you least expect it.

Defensive ends can be made conscious of the bootleg if you condition them to vocally proclaim on every play, "I got the bootleg." They might not get the bootleg everytime, but they will always be aware of it, and the offense will be conscious that someone on the defense is responsible for the bootleg.

In addition to being aware of the bootleg, you must defend

it. An ideal way to protect against the bootleg is to send your end through the backfield whenever the play goes the opposite way (see Figure 4-7). When he goes through the backfield, he must be neither too deep nor too shallow. If he is too deep, the play can come back inside him. If he is too shallow, the bootleg can go around him. A good angle would take the end through the position where the near offensive halfback would align. However, you are safer having your end go shallow than deep because this would cause the bootleg to go deeper, giving the defense time to recover.

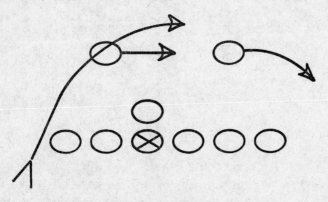

Figure 4-7

The defender responsible for the bootleg should not pursue the play on the opposite side until he clearly sees the ball two yards across the line of scrimmage. When the ball is at this point, it is safe for the offside end to pursue the play downfield. This technique of defending the bootleg will cost you some pursuit, but it will save you some sleep.

Pursuing Inside Plays

The inside pursuit you get from your defensive end is determined by whether your end plays pressure or contain. If your end is playing a pressure end without contain responsibility, he can give you more pressure inside. If he has outside responsibility, you are not going to get as much pursuit from him inside.

A defensive end can safely pursue an inside play when he clearly sees the ball on the defensive side of the line of scrimmage (see Figure 4-8). He should angle for a position one yard in front of the ball carrier.

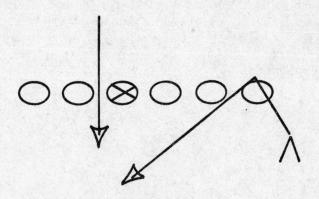

Figure 4-8

Pressure type ends usually have some off-tackle responsibility. They can pursue inside better than contain ends can pursue in that area. Pressure ends normally have more responsibility off-tackle since someone else has outside contain.

Pressure ends can read inside plays by keying the block of the offensive man on whom they align. If their man blocks down, the defensive end can close down and get a jump on inside pursuit.

Playing Pass Responsibilities

Pursuing inside and outside plays is difficult for defensive ends, but playing pass responsibilities is a more difficult part of their job. The skill of the defensive end is shown when he is called upon to drop back and play pass defense.

Many defensive ends will not have a defensive back's agility to drop back and cover pass, so you should make their drop as easy as possible. Using sound techniques will make your teaching as easy as possible.

Before your end drops, he must read a pass key. Common pass keys for defensive ends are:

1. The offensive end releasing downfield
2. The offensive tackle showing pass block
3. The near back releasing for a pattern or pass blocking
4. The quarterback dropping back
5. Game conditions—score, situation, time, and so forth

When the key is recognized, there are two common theories on how to drop into the pass area:

1. Take a cross-over step and sprint back while looking at the eyes of the passer
2. Back-pedalling, also looking at the passer while dropping.

The first method is naturally quicker, but the second allows the end to maintain better vision with the passer.

As the drop is made into the assigned area, the end has to read every key available to get the direction of the ball. The major key as he drops is the eyes of the passer. If the passer looks in the end's area, he must further discern the location of the receiver. A good scouting report will help the end recognize favorite short patterns in his area. The defender can use sound and sight to find a receiver in his area; sight of the receiver's shadow can also be a key to locating him.

In conclusion, defensive end is the most difficult defensive line position to play. He has more area to protect than any other defensive lineman. More responsibilities cause him to know more techniques than other defensive linemen. He must know techniques for pass rush as well as pass drop. He must be able to pursue the run inside and the run outside. While pursuing inside and outside, he must avoid being hooked and tricked on such plays as bootlegs and reverses.

The defensive end's responsibilities must be further refined according to your individual philosophy. Your personal defense will dictate the execution of such skills as crashing, pressuring, and containing. Good defensive ends can make an average defense good.

DRILLS

1. Goal Post Drill.

Purpose: To react on movement. To make contact with the offensive man while in the up position.

Procedure: Defensive ends align on each side of goal post. Reacting to movement, they take their first step with up foot, their second step with back foot, and their third step with their back foot (see Figure 4-9). With their last step, they make solid contact against the goal post with heels of the hands.

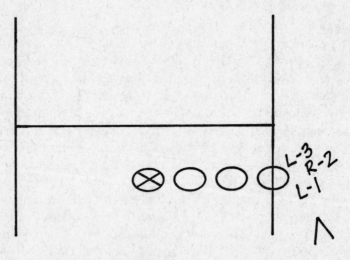

Figure 4-9

Comment: This drill teaches the proper up-stance with the inside foot up. The steps may seem awkward at first, but repetition will make them rhythmical. Defensive ends should practice this drill from both sides since the lead foot is different from each side.

2. Hook-Release Drill.

Purpose: To teach the defensive end to distinguish between an outside release and hook.

Procedure: Defensive ends align one-on-one with offensive ends. Ends try to either hook the defensive end or release downfield. The defensive end must keep his hands in front of him to avoid the offensive man from getting into his body. The defender can use the key described in Chapter 3. When the offensive man's helmet is low, he is going to hook. When the offensive man's helmet is high, he is going to release downfield.

3. "Ball Comes, I Come; Ball Goes, I Go."

Purpose: To teach the defensive end to react to ball keys when the ball comes to his side.

Procedure: Defensive ends align on offensive ends and a skeleton backfield. The end keys the movement of the ball. When the ball comes to the end (back off tackle), the defensive end comes up to meet him. When the ball goes away (roll-out, quick pitch, dropback pass), the defensive end goes away from the ball and gets to his responsibility.

4. Cut 'em Off at the Pass.

Purpose: To teach proper angle of pursuit on outside plays. To learn to adjust speed and angle according to the speed of the back.

Procedure: Defensive ends line up in normal position. Offensive backs line up with ball in the position of the near half. When back is ready, he starts to run wide. Defensive end takes necessary angle of pursuit to cut off back (see Figure 4-10).

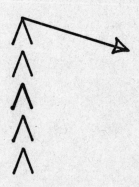

Figure 4-10

5

Recognizing
Special Plays

Stopping screens. Diverting draws. Terminating traps. Keying counters.

At night following a close loss, certain plays seem to produce nightmares. These game-breaking plays are: screens, draws, traps, and counters.

These four types of plays are designed to trick defenses by getting them to think one play is developing and then running another. These plays are even more difficult to defend when your opponent successfully runs the basic initial action of the play. In other words, a team's success to screen and draw is determined by their ability to pass. Their ability to trap generally is determined by their success to run outside and their success to counter is controlled by their ability to run directly at the defense.

The success of the basic plays directly affects the success of the take-off plays. When the basic plays are successful, the trick plays will soon follow. To successfully defend against these game-breaking plays, you must teach your linemen to recognize the keys to these plays. Once the keys are recognized, your defensive linemen must be taught how to react to them and stop the play.

Stopping Screens

The objective of the offense when they run a screen play is to get the defensive linemen in a position where they are totally ineffective—halfway between the passer and the receiver. When the defensive linemen are in this position, they can neither rush the passer nor get to the receiver.

The best defense against the screen is to recognize the keys to screen plays and stop a problem before it begins. When your defensive linemen learn to recognize and defend screen plays, you won't have to worry about stopping the big play, and you can be worrying about what to run for the conversion play.

Common keys to recognize the screen are the following:

1. Situation
2. Quarterback dropping extra deep
3. Quarterback back-pedalling when he usually uses a cross-over step
4. Defensive line meeting little or no resistance
5. Two or more linemen going into flat
6. A back flaring into the flat

The most obvious key to a screen is a passing situation. When down and distance indicate pass, linemen should instinctively think screen and draw. A summary of the more than 500 games that we have scouted indicates that the most likely down to screen is second—particularly, second and long yardage. The same statistics indicate that the least likely situation to screen is first and ten. An exception is a repeated first down that follows a fifteen yard penalty. Field situation analysis from scouting the same number of games shows the area between the 30's is the area where the screen is most likely to be thrown.

Your weekly scouting reports may indicate a formation tendency for the screen play, as well as the situation and field position. You may also discover that your opponent has a favorite screen back and/or a favorite screen side. Some teams have a tendency to screen to the wide side of the field. If you're especially observant, you may pick up a coach's tendency to call screens to his side of the field so that he may better see the play.

In addition to the side screens, the middle screen is becoming a popular offensive weapon because coaches and defenders are conditioned to think outside when they think screen. The infrequency of opponents to use the middle screen adds to the problem of defending it. We will find the middle screen easier to defend when offenses use it more often. An irony of offensive football is that popularity leads to a lack of effectiveness.

In addition to the situation key for the outside screen as well as the middle screen, the quarterback's dropping extra deep is a key for both screens. This key is easily recognizable to offensive linemen because few offensive plays require the quarterback to be back more than eight to ten yards. The extra depth should trigger defensive linemen to think trick.

Some quarterbacks further key their drops by back-pedalling on screens so they maintain vision with the receiver. You should look for this key when you scout. You will be fortunate if you notice that the passer back-pedals exclusively on screens.

Another key of this type is that the quarterback will always look in the opposite direction from the screen or he will drop in a slight roll away from the direction of the screen.

The offensive linemen also provide a screen key on initial contact or the lack of initial contact. In passing situations, defensive linemen must learn to "feel" little or no resistance from offensive linemen. Since this reduction of the initial hit is such a contrast to normal contact, defensive linemen should be alerted for a trick.

Poor contact by the offensive line may be read as a trap or missed blocking assignment or an off-side play, but when the key is read with linemen going into the flat, the defender has an additional indication of a screen play. Your defensive linemen can read the pulling offensive linemen as a directional key unless your opponent has shown a screen play off a fake screen to the opposite side (see Figure 5-1).

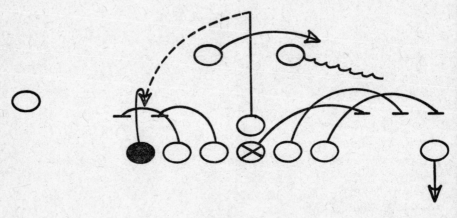

Figure 5-1

The key of the linemen going out to the flat is usually coupled with a back also going out—especially if he is a back to whom your opponent likes to screen. Offensive backs who receive screen passes are taught to fake a block and then slide into the flat. Since most offensive teams don't practice screen plays as much as they practice other plays, the unskilled back usually rushes the fake block and hustles into the flat waving his arms, showing how open he is and telling the defense a screen is developing.

Recognizing the back in the flat and the other keys for a screen play is the first step in preventing the play. The second step is the only step that's important—stopping the screen.

We prefer to give the primary screen responsibility to our outside pass rushers, the down end linemen. Our inside rushers are primarily responsible for the draw.

All defensive linemen should use one or more of the keys to anticipate the screen and avoid being caught between the passer and the receiver. If defensive linemen successfully read the screen and avoid being caught halfway, one of them has an opportunity not only to break up the screen, but also to intercept the pass with an unobstructed path to the goal line.

When the screen pass is successfully read, the defender should approach the screen receiver on an angle similar to an angle of pursuit for an outside play (see Figure 5-2). As soon as the lineman recognizes the screen, he should sprint for a position about one yard in front of the receiver. When he gets there, he has the added insurance of knowing that he is permitted to make contact with the receiver, as long as the receiver is behind the line of scrimmage. The rules permit the defender to literally knock down the receiver and catch the ball. For the defender to do this, the receiver must be behind the line of scrimmage where screen plays are designed to be thrown. From your experience, you know that high school plays don't always end up the way they're drawn up.

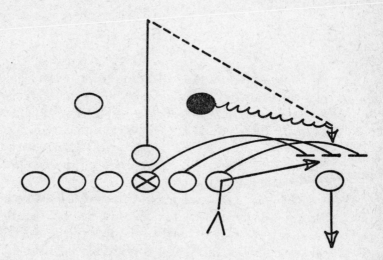

Figure 5-2

Sometimes an unsuccessful screen pass can result in a defensive score if your linemen are alert. A poorly timed screen pass is sometimes thrown when the receiver is farther back than the passer (see Figure 5-3). This causes the ball to be thrown backwards. A backwards pass (once referred to as a lateral), whether complete or incomplete, is a live ball and can be advanced by the defense (American Federation Rules). Your players can be alerted to this type of situation by the absence of a whistle to stop the play when the screen pass is not successfully completed. Your opponent's failure to complete can be converted into your success.

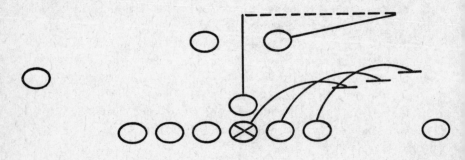

Figure 5-3

When you practice defending screen plays, condition your players to defend with total success—a score. Practice success to the point of what to do with the ball after scoring (hand it to the nearest official) and what to do to celebrate the score (within the limits of what you permit after a score). Our scoring tradition is that a lineman who scores is carried off the field following the first practice after the game.

To score on a screen play, three areas must be blocked (see Figure 5-4). One critical block must be made on the intended receiver. The receiver is the first person who has to be blocked on any interception. Another critical block must be made on the passer, who is usually the only obstacle between the intercepter and the goal line. The last critical block must be made in the area of the center of the original line of scrimmage. This is the most concentrated area of the opposition, and some pursuit usually comes from here.

In addition to having specific assignments to defend the outside screen, linemen must have specific responsibilities to defend the middle screen. The defensive danger of the middle

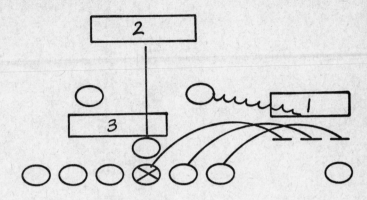

Figure 5-4

screen and the offensive advantage it has over the outside screen
is that the receiver catches the ball with a direct path to the goal
line and with the entire offensive line in front of him and possibly with the entire defensive line in back of him.

Successful defense of the middle screen is determined by
early recognition. Once a successful middle screen starts, stopping it is a problem. You will find it much easier to stop a middle
screen before it starts rather than after it starts.

To stop this play before it starts, we have occasionally assigned a defensive lineman to stay home on the rush and watch
specifically for this play. Your scouting report will give you an
indication of the effectiveness of your opponent's middle screen.
You may also find a tendency for the middle screen to be thrown
to a favorite receiver. It can be thrown to a halfback, slotback or
wingback, or a tight end.

To defend the middle screen, no matter whom it's intended
for, some linemen must pressure the passer to make him get rid
of the ball quickly. Other defensive linemen who recognize the
middle screen more quickly should do an about face and head
directly for the receiver (see Figure 5-5). Unrealistically, if all
rushing linemen recognized the middle screen, they would all
be waiting for the quarterback's pass—along with the receiver.
But, boys being boys, some will read screen and some will rush
the passer. The "slow readers" will defend the receiver. If the
ultimate did occur and the complete defensive line did read

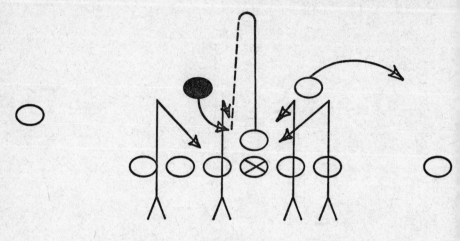

Figure 5-5

screen, there would be no threat of a quarterback scramble because all run areas would be covered.

When the middle screen receiver is being chased from the rear, he is vulnerable to fumbling on the tackle because he doesn't have time to prepare for the rear hit. Defenders should tackle the middle screen receiver using the same technique as tackling the quarterback from the blind side—attack the football. This technique gives your defender an opportunity to stop a potentially big offensive play and start a potentially big defensive play.

Diverting Draws

Whenever your defensive linemen think screen, they should also think draw. Keys that will alert them to draws include the following:

1. Situation
2. Field position
3. Formation tendency
4. The quarterback showing the ball
5. The back holding his hands in position to receive the ball

6. Eye contact between the quarterback and the draw back
7. The back giving an early fake of a block
8. The back chopping in place

The situation key for the two plays is essentially the same—long yardage.

In scouting offensive tendencies we have discovered that the most frequent situation for the draw is third and long. This is followed by second and long and finally first and ten. Most high school teams are unlikely to screen and draw on first and ten, but they are more likely to draw than screen.

Field situation analysis over the same period of games shows that draws are more likely to be run where screens are not likely to be run—inside the 20 at both ends of the field. This is because of the relative safety of the draw as compared with the screen.

Similar to the screen, an offensive team is likely to have a favorite draw back. Frequently, you will find a favorite draw formation. Most draws are designed to run up the middle. This middle tendency affords your defensive linemen the key of the offensive blocking pressure being from the inside to the outside (see Figure 5-6). This occurs when offensive linemen drop inside while showing pass and encourages defensive linemen to take the outside where they can be taken farther out.

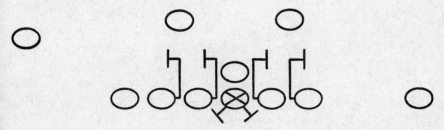

Figure 5-6

These keys will help give your linemen early recognition for the draw, but recognition doesn't stop the draw—making the tackle stops the draw. The best way to stop the draw is to pass

rush directly to the blocking backs (see Figure 5-7), because if
the play is a draw, one of those backs will have the ball.

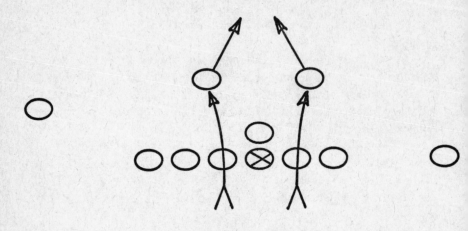

Figure 5-7

While rushing to the blocking back, defensive linemen may
read a draw key that is given by many inexperienced quarterbacks: showing the ball on the way back to the draw back. When
the quarterback shows the ball high in the air, the defensive
linemen should imagine him to be holding up a giant sign that
says draw.

Your linemen may get an additional key if the quarterback
maintains a strong eye fixation with the back who is getting the
ball. Occasionally, the draw back will fake the block, positioning
his hands to receive the hand-off and chopping his feet in place.

When a defensive lineman reads draw and rushes to the
draw back, he should make contact with that draw back so that
he does not over-penetrate the back. He must also make sure
that he is in position to stop or upset the timing of the draw
hand-off.

Making contact with the blocking back can sometimes prevent or delay the draw, but occasionally the hand-off will be
successfully made. When the back gets the ball, defensive linemen must get to him as soon as possible. The angle of pursuit is

similar to that of a middle screen, a straight line charge from the rear (see Figure 5-8). Successful draw pursuit is predicated on recognizing that a draw has developed and making an about face to get a good start. This technique can stop the big play.

Figure 5-8

Terminating Traps

Another big play that you must defend is the trap. Similar to the screen and draw, a successful trap play capitalizes on over-aggressiveness by the defenders. Terminating the trap is similar to stopping the screen and diverting the draw—early recognition and quick reaction.

Early recognition of the trap is determined by how well your linemen read the following keys for the trap play:

1. Situation
2. Reading the offensive man for a pull
3. Little or no pressure from the offensive man
4. The quarterback showing the ball on the fake pitch
5. The fake pitch back showing no ball

Our scouting tendencies have shown that more traps are

run on first downs than any other down. Naturally, the frequency of traps depends on the type of offense a team is running and the effectiveness of their outside game to set up the trap. With the exception of predominately trap offenses (Pro, Wing T, and so forth), traps are intended to be the big play. Usually, if you can stop the trap early in the game, the offense will assume that the trap is closed and not return to it later in the game.

Your scouting report will tell you specifically when to expect the trap, but generally you can expect it when a team is running outside and they are looking for a change-up. The trap is set up by conditioning defensive linemen to pursue to the outside. Then when they move out too quickly, the trap back comes back inside and the defender is out of position.

Defensive linemen can avoid being out of position by reading the alignment of their offensive man for a trap key. There are two offensive linemen who can give a trap key—the set-up man and the trapper. An offensive man can key that he is pulling (for a trap or sweep) by giving any one of the following keys:

1. Cheating his split to get closer to the man whom he is trapping (see Figure 5-9)

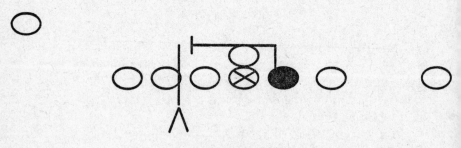

Figure 5-9

2. Pointing his stance in the direction of his pull
3. Lining up back a little farther to make the pull easier (see Figure 5-10)

The offensive man who is setting up the trap man may indicate his intentions by one of the following:

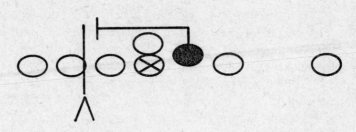

Figure 5-10

1. Trying to force the defender to his outside (see Figure 5-11)

2. Trying to get the defender to come up high, making him more vulnerable to the block

Figure 5-11

Regardless of how the trap man is set up, very little contact will be made with him. The offensive lineman does not want to get tied up with him at the line of scrimmage. The offense wants the defender to get a yard or more into the offensive backfield. The deeper the defensive man penetrates, the easier he will be blocked.

Your defensive linemen must be able to "feel" the lack of pressure to recognize the trap play that is developing. His total awareness of available keys will help him discern whether the play is a trap, draw, screen, or something other.

Another key that will help a defensive lineman specifically read trap is the quarterback showing the ball when he makes a fake quick pitch. When your defensive linemen see the ball on the fake quick pitch, they have a reliable trap key.

Your scouting report must make your linemen aware of the area where your opponent traps—on the front side of the quarterback (see Figure 5-12) or the back side of the quarterback (see Figure 5-13). Very few teams run traps with the quarterback sometimes making a front trap hand-off and sometimes making a back hand-off. Another strongly reliable key for the trap is the fake pitch back showing his hands and clearly indicating that he doesn't have the ball.

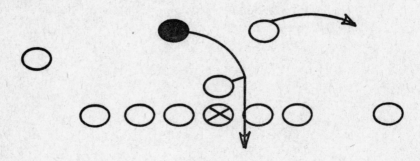

Figure 5-12

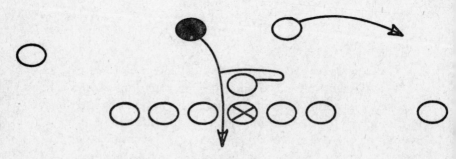

Figure 5-13

All the mentioned trap keys will give your defensive linemen an indication of what play is developing, but the important part of defense is stopping the play. There are two common techniques to use to avoid being trapped:

1. Drop to all fours and overturn the trapper with a shoulder shiver.
2. Use a shoulder block to redirect the force of the trapper into the hole (see Figure 5-14).

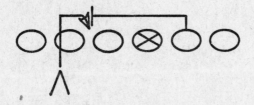

Figure 5-14

Dropping to all fours will place the defender in a position that makes him extremely difficult to be blocked. The offensive lineman is not likely to get under the defender because he is on all fours and the blocker will be running in an upright position. The shoulder block is another good technique to use to defend against the trapper. The defensive man must make contact towards the back shoulder of the blocker. The defensive man must redirect the path of the offensive man into the hole that the blocker is trying to open.

Keying Counters

Another type of play that attempts to deceive the defense is the counter. Counters are misdirections of basic plays. They do not try to fool the defense as much as the screens and draws; they merely try to get the defense a step or two out of position. Once they get a defender out of position, they come back and run the play at the location where the defender just vacated. Sometimes counters are run with a trap block at the point of attack.

Counters can be run from almost any backfield set. The ball carrier can be one of the set backs or a wing back. Counters

usually include crossing action in the backfield. The problem
this presents for the defense is determining who has the ball.
When a third back is involved in the action, the problem for the
defense becomes more complicated.

As previously mentioned, early recognition is the key to
defending this type of play. Common keys for recognizing counters include the following:

1. Crossing action in the backfield
2. A fake jab step by the tailback in an "I" set
3. A pulling lineman with the backs crossing
4. A wingback cheating to the inside

If you are fortunate, you may find a sure counter key when
offensive backs cross. When most teams cross backs, the second
back usually gets the ball. Your linemen will have less difficulty
with counters if they know that whenever backs cross, the second back will have the ball. A priority when you scout should be
to find out if your opponent has a play where they cross the
backs and give the ball to the first man through. If they run this
play, the counter will be more difficult to defend.

Counters from the "I" formation are more difficult to defend because the crossing action with either back carrying the
ball is more common to that offense. An occasional counter key
from the "I" that we have used is the tailback taking a short jab
step in the opposite direction of which he is carrying the ball (see
Figure 5-15). Both these actions may or may not include a pulling lineman.

If you are fortunate, you may get an alignment key or a
pointing key by the wingback. The fewer keys you have on an
opponent, the more time you must use to condition your defensive linemen to seeing this play.

The first defense to reading the counter is for the defensive
linemen to key the men in their area. This was discussed in
detail in Chapter 3. After reading the offensive men in his area,
the defensive lineman can read the cross of the backs. If the
scouting report shows that they only cross with the second back
getting the ball, the defensive linemen can hold their ground

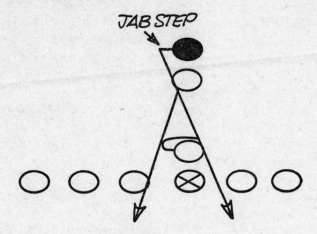

Figure 5-15

while the offensive backs are crossing. If the linemen do not have the luxury of this key, they must use another key or do their best to find the ball.

If your opponent runs the counter with a pulling guard, your lineman will be in a position to defend it by reacting to the pull, whether it be for trap or counter. If the wingback is involved in the counter, your defensive linemen must be alerted to the first sign of the wingback coming to the inside. Your defensive tackle or end must alert the other linemen of a back coming to the inside. A call alerting them to a reverse will enable them to change their direction or hold their ground.

When our tackles alert the defense of the wingback coming to the inside, we prefer him to make a one syllable call "verse" rather than making a two syllable call "reverse." The shorter call "verse" enables the defense to react more quickly than "reverse" where the first syllable "re" doesn't mean anything to the defense.

When the defense hears the "verse" call, they should change direction and look for the play to be behind them. With the exception of the Wing T Offense, very few offensive plays are designed with the wingback going inside and not getting the ball.

If the defense doesn't have a key to use to read the wing-back counter, they must read the lack of pressure in the direction in which they are headed. If they meet no resistance on their way to the ball carrier, they must know to change direction because they are not going to be in the play.

In conclusion, the key to stopping special plays is early recognition. The earlier the play is recognized, the less likely that it will develop into a big play. Your players will recognize these plays when they become familiar with the keys that indicate each play.

You will have a back-up defense for these plays when your defense knows what to do when the plays begin to successfully develop. Being fully prepared for these plays will give you a better defense and a better sleep.

DRILLS

1. Screen/Draw Drill.

Purpose: To read and react to screens and draws.

Procedure: Defensive linemen react to an offense that runs screens and draws exclusively.

Comment: Emphasize execution of individual coaching skills that are discussed in Chapter 5.

2. Screen Keys.

Purpose: To develop defensive reactions to individual screen keys.

Procedure: Defensive linemen react to individual screen keys.

Comment: The whole/part whole teaching technique is generally accepted as extremely effective. The reactions to individual keys follow reactions to the play as a whole.

3. Draw Keys.

This drill is similar to the Screen Keys Drill.

4. Trap/Pitch Drill.

Basic idea is similar to the Screen/Draw Drill.

5. Trap Keys Drill.

(Keys are discussed in Chapter 5.)

6. Counter Keys Drill.

(Keys are discussed in Chapter 5.)

6

Rushing the Passer

Teaching rush techniques. Playing pass defense up front. Defending action passes.

As the high school passing game becomes more developed and diversified, the defense against the pass must be equally developed and diversified.

Pass defense begins up front with a good rush. We all know the feeling of looking downfield and seeing a receiver in the clear, and then looking at the quarterback and seeing him sacked.

The chances of seeing your opponent's quarterback sacked increase as your defensive linemen become more skilled at rushing the passer. The amount of time you practice pass rushing skills should be commensurate with your opponent's ability to throw the ball. Pass rush time should vary from week to week.

Teaching Rush Techniques

Before your lineman uses a rush technique, he must recognize that the play is a pass. Pass keys are discussed at length in Chapter 1, but in summary they are:

1. Long yardage for the first down
2. Your opponent trailing and time running out
3. Your lineman's man leaning back in his stance with little pressure on his fingers, his heels on the ground, and a bend in the elbow so he can push back

When these keys are not available, your lineman must wait until he recognizes more obvious keys:

1. The offensive lineman pass blocking
2. The quarterback going back to pass
3. Backs setting up to pass block

When the pass key becomes reality, linemen should make a call (usually "pass") to alert the other members of the defense and then expect a fake off the pass, such as a screen or draw. Your scouting report should alert them to expect any other un- usual plays such as: the Statue of Liberty, reverse (see Figure 6-1), double pass, quarterback draw, draw hand-off from behind the back (see Figure 6-2), middle screen, screen off a fake screen, and so forth.

After the pass is recognized and the fake is checked, the defensive lineman has two objectives:

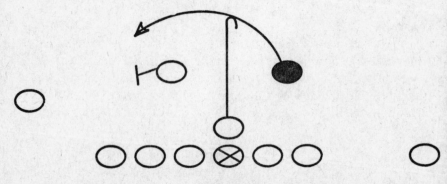

Figure 6-1

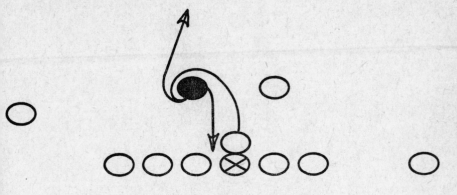

Figure 6-2

1. Get past the opponent as quickly as possible
2. Get to the quarterback or make it as difficult as possible.
for him to throw the ball.

To achieve the first of these objectives, your linemen should be familiar with various pass rush techniques.

Spins

The objective of the spins is for the defender to use the momentum from the initial charge and maneuver around the man, using a final push off him to get additional momentum to get to the passer.

A spin is executed by placing the near side foot (foot on side to which your defensive man is spinning) in a triangle with the feet of the offensive man (see Figure 6-3). As soon as the foot is positioned, the head and far elbow are thrown around in the direction of the spin (see Figure 6-4).

Similar to initial charge techniques, the head establishes the path for which the remainder of the body follows. If the head is slow, the whole body will be slow.

The flailing of the opposite elbow gives momentum to the spin and clears a path for the spin. During the spin, your defensive man should keep body contact with his man. This is important for these reasons:

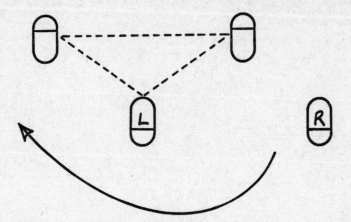

Figure 6-3

Figure 6-4

1. It keeps him in his pass rushing lane.
2. It keeps him away from blocks by other offensive men.
3. It keeps him in position to push off the offensive man so that he can gain additional speed to get to the passer.

Maintaining body contact permits the defender to know where the offensive man is located so that at the conclusion of the spin, the defensive lineman can continue the moving of the flailing arm and place it on the tail of the offensive man. With the hand on the offensive man, the defender can push off to the direction of the passer.

Beating a Shoulder

The objective of beating a shoulder is to get the offensive man in a position so that one of his shoulders is turned back. Once the offensive man is in this position, the defensive man can get a shoulder past the offensive man's turned shoulder and the offender will not be in a position to block the defender.

There are three common techniques for turning the shoulder of the offensive man:

1. Push and pull
2. Swim
3. Handlebar grab

The "push and pull" technique is executed by having your defender place the heel of one hand under one side of the man's shoulder pads and the other hand behind the shoulder on the other side (see Figure 6-5). The hands can easily push and pull the opponent's shoulders, causing one of the shoulders to turn backwards.

When one of the opponent's shoulders is turned back, your defensive lineman must bring up his arm so that the back of his shoulder is against the turned shoulder of the offensive man. When your defensive lineman gets to this position, the offensive man can offer little resistance between himself and the passer. Also, once the defender gets his shoulder against the offensive man, the offender is in the precarious position of blocking the back of the defender, causing a clip.

Figure 6-5

The "swim" technique is another method of getting past the
offensive man's shoulder. To execute this technique, the defender raises his arm over the top in a swimming motion and
positions it in front of one of the offender's shoulders (see Figure
6-6). The swimming arm is continued down so that the hand is
placed on the back of the man. From this position the defender
can push off to the direction of the passer.

The "handlebar grab" is another way to get past the shoulder of the offensive man. It can be executed only when the
offensive man uses a poor blocking technique and blocks with his
elbows held high like handlebars on a bicycle. The handlebars
can be twisted, similar to the push and pull technique, and the
offensive man is in good position to be beaten through one of his
turned shoulders.

Figure 6-6

Fakes

A variation of the spins and beating a shoulder is the fakes. Faking to one side and going to the other is a good change-up to beat an intelligent offensive lineman who can read the spins and the beating of a shoulder.

Faking off the spin is executed by taking a short step in the opposite direction with the lead foot (the right foot for a fake right and spin left). The other foot forms a triangle with the feet of the offensive man (see Figure 6-7). The defender then spins back away from his initial lead foot, using the original spin technique. The spin off beating a shoulder is executed by faking to beat a shoulder to one side and spinning back the opposite way.

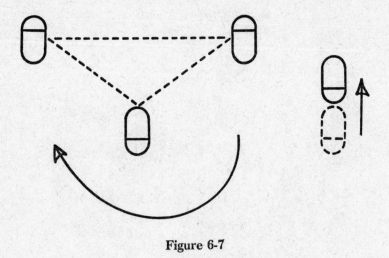

Figure 6-7

When you teach a variety of pass rush techniques, you are developing defensive linemen with diversified skills. You are giving them a wide selection of techniques from which they can develop their speciality.

Playing Pass Defense Up Front

You are aware of the importance of playing pass defense up front—your first line of pass defense, but you must be sure to develop your defensive linemen with pass defense skills that complement the pass defense skills you teach to your secondary. In other words, if you expect your defensive backs to get to the ball when it is in the air, you must teach your defensive linemen to cause the ball to be in the air as long as possible.

Pass defense up front begins with a good rush, and a good rush begins with recognizing the pass, checking for the fake off the pass, and quickly getting past the blocker. Once past the blocker, your defensive lineman can be of direct value to the secondary by causing the passer to do something that he is unprepared to do.

Effective pass defense up front includes forcing the passer to do one or more of the following:

1. Get the attention of the rusher, causing the passer to take his eye off the receivers.

2. Throw from another location, other than where he was originally prepared to throw.

3. Think about the rusher instead of thinking about passing the ball.

4. Release the ball at a time other than when he wants to release it.

5. Release the ball from a position other than where he wants to release it—specifically, releasing the ball higher so it will be in the air longer, giving the secondary more time to react.

6. Throw the ball away.

7. Get sacked.

8. Fumble the ball.

To force one or more of the above goals, the rusher must remain in his rushing lane (see Figure 6-8). All your defenses should include inside pass pressure, outside pass pressure, and outside contain pressure. Some defenses are designed with the outside pressure also being the contain. Rushing lanes are protection against the run if the passer doesn't pass. The lanes also provide even pressure inside and outside.

The closer the rushers get to the passer, the more effective they will be. Once near the passer, linemen should raise their finger tips. They can get additional height by jumping. Your linemen can better time their jumps by going up when the passer makes a forward motion with his throwing shoulder. High school quarterbacks can usually pump fake with their arms and elbows, but few of them can pump fake with their shoulders.

When defensive linemen approach the passer with the

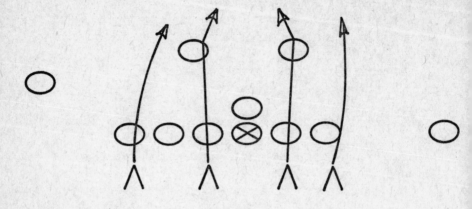

Figure 6-8

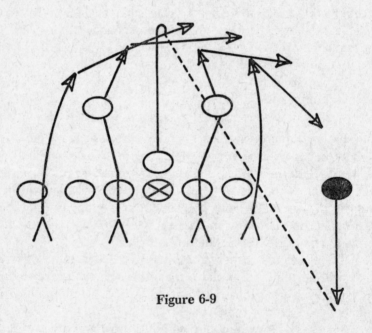

Figure 6-9

fingertips up, they are in position to tackle the passer from the top down. Tackling high gives the passer the least amount of time to throw the ball, and it increases the chances of a fumble.

When a defensive lineman has an opportunity to tackle the passer from the blind side, he should go directly for the ball. If the passer successfully releases the ball, the defensive linemen's job is not complete—they should move in the direction of the ball in anticipation of an interception (see Figure 6-9). Also, this movement will put them closer to the ball should it be tipped. In addition, it will make them conscious of an interception on every pass and further train them to play offensive defense.

Defending Action Passes

The most difficult type of pass to defend is the action pass. These passes are not only difficult to defend up front, but are also difficult in the secondary. They are a problem to defend up front because defensive linemen must first defend the run and when a play initially looks like a run, defensive linemen first think of defending their primary responsibility.

Similar to defending other types of difficult plays, the key to defending action passes is early recognition. Unlike other types of trick plays, once the action pass develops, it is very difficult to defend.

Keys that will help your linemen recognize an action pass include the following:

1. A scouting report tendency
2. Passing situations
3. An unaggressive uncovered offensive lineman on either side of the defensive man
4. An offensive back, pulling up short on a fake
5. A back without the ball trying to get through the line

The importance of using scouting report tendencies cannot be overemphasized. Your report will not only tell you "what," "who," "when," and "where," it will also keep you conscious of the plays that you must defend. Plays that appear frequently in your scouting report will be foremost in the minds of your players.

You are not likely to get strong tendencies on your oppo-

nent's action passes because they are not likely to throw that
many. However, the number of action passes they throw will tell
you how much time you must spend preparing for them. You
cannot be well prepared for an action pass every running situation, but you can expect an action pass every passing situation.

Action passes are more difficult to read in running situations, and defensive linemen have to rely on keys other than the
situation. One of those keys is an uncovered lineman holding his
position on the line so that he isn't downfield on the pass. Some
inexperienced linemen may even show a pass block rather than
an aggressive block.

In addition to offensive linemen keying action passes, the
backs can also key the play. A common backfield key is for the
offensive back to pull up short on the fake while the quarterback
is looking for the intended receiver. Some offensive patterns call
for the backs to cross on an action pass, and the cross is commonly more of a flat cross (see Figure 6-10) than a deep cross.

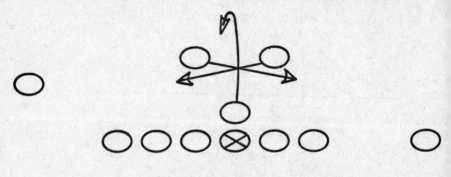

Figure 6-10

Sometimes backs will try to get through the line to be the
intended receiver of the action pass. A general rule for defensive
linemen is not to let any back get cleanly through the line.

If the offensive backs and other keys do not give early recognition of the action pass, there is very little that you can do to
stop the ball from being thrown. As a last resort, your defensive
linemen can raise their fingertips when they recognize the ac-

tion pass being thrown. However, don't be annoyed if your linemen don't always have their hands up on action passes because offensive linemen are drilled on action passes to fire out at the knees of defensive linemen. This causes your linemen to instinctively reach down to protect their knees rather than reach up to defend the action pass. If the action pass is long, your defensive linemen can use a pass rush technique after they recognize the pass.

In conclusion, the more pass defense you play up front, the less you will have to play in the secondary. Also, you will have a greater margin of available error in the secondary. You can reduce the pressure on your secondary by quickly getting to the passer and upsetting the timing of the pass play. Only when you perfect your upfront pass skills, will the pass protection of your secondary be truly secondary.

DRILLS

1. Numbers Game.

Purpose: To teach individual segments of skills.

Procedure: Each defensive player has an offensive partner. You select a skill that you wish to teach, for example, the push and pull pass rush technique. Divide the technique into the individual segments: hand position, twisting, shooting the shoulder past, and so forth. As you call out a number, defensive linemen perform one of the segments.

Comments: This is a basic drill for introducing a basic skill. The complete skill is easier to teach when the players know the individual parts. The complete skill cannot be correctly executed unless the players can successfully perform the individual parts.

2. Net Drill.

Purpose: To keep rushers in their passing lanes and show them how much of the hook zone they can take away when they raise their fingertips.

Procedure: Defensive linemen stand in their lane, with their fingertips in front of the passer (see Figure 6-11). The passer throws the ball over their tips. Defensive linemen recognize how much of the hook zone cannot be thrown to because the ball must travel over their fingertips.

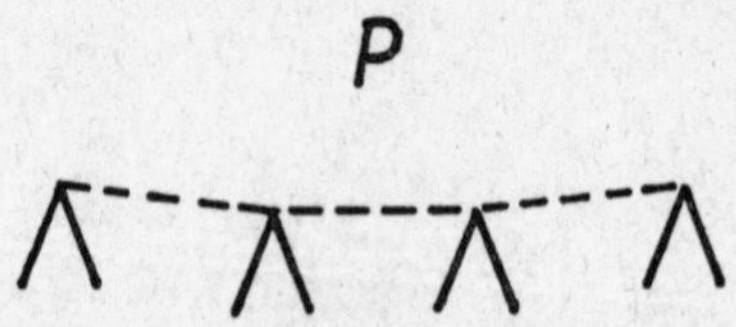

Figure 6-11

Comments: This drill represents an ideal situation, but defensive linemen will get the idea of how their extended fingertips cause the ball to be in the air longer and how they block the ball from being thrown to certain areas.

3. Pump Fake Drill.

Purpose: To teach defensive linemen to jump when the throwing shoulder comes forward and not to jump on the pump fake.

Procedure: Defender stands directly in front of the passer. Passer pump fakes and throws. Defender jumps only when the throwing shoulder moves forward.

Comments: Type of pump fake should vary each week according to the type of fake that is used by the opponent's passer.

4. Block the Shot Drill.

Purpose: To develop the skill of blocking a pass and possibly catching the pass immediately after it is thrown.

Procedure: A defensive lineman stands in front of a passer with his fingertips up. The passer is on one knee. The passer throws the ball into the hands of the defender. The defender gets the feeling of batting the ball and occasionally he will catch the ball. The action of the lineman is similar to blocking a basketball shot.

Comments: Defensive linemen take pride in any drill where they can show their ball handling ability. Causing a tip or batting the ball from the passer is a way that they can stand out among their peers.

5. Rapid Fire Technique Drill.

Purpose: To give repetitions in teaching one skill or a number of skills.

Procedure: A defensive player stands in front of a line of about five offensive players who are about four yards apart (see

Figure 6-12) and in a pass blocking position. The defensive man approaches each offensive man and executes the same defensive skill such as the pass rushing spins, or the defensive man uses a different skill on each offensive man.

Figure 6-12

Comments: This is a basic drill for teaching the techniques, or it can be used as a drill to sharpen skills that are previously known.

6. Blind Side Strip Drill.

Purpose: To develop the skill of attacking the ball from the blind side of the passer and reinforce the philosophy of teaching offensive defense.

Procedure: The passer stands with the ball in the throwing position and with his back to the pass rusher. The defender attacks the ball, causes the fumble, and scores with the ball.

Comments: Common sense dictates that you don't run this drill live. You want to give the defender the idea of attacking the ball from the blind side, causing the fumble, and scoring. The drill does not necessitate aggressive contact with the passer.

7

Getting Defensive Linemen to the Ball

Releasing to get to the ball.   Shedding.   Tackling.

Whether the play is a pass or run, defensive linemen cannot do their job successfully unless they get to the ball. Getting defensive linemen to the ball would be an easy task if it weren't for the fact that the job of the offense is to prevent the defense from getting there. Since the offense is uncooperative with the defensive duty, we must be prepared with releases that permit the defense to get started in the direction of the ball.

Once defensive linemen are free from the offensive block, they must take the shortest path to be where the ball carrier will be. If opposition is encountered along the way, shedding techniques must be employed to prevent delay.

When all resistance is overcome, defensive linemen are ready to achieve their ultimate—stop the progress of the ball carrier.

Releasing to Get to the Ball

Similar to rushing the passer, the best release technique depends on what the offensive player takes away and what the defensive player does best. The defensive player must use the easiest release that is given to him by the offense. Therefore, he must be familiar with a number of techniques. The following releases will allow him to escape from almost any offensive situation.

Push and Open Step

This type of release is the most obvious. It is used when the offensive man has little or no control of the defender and when the offensive man's head is on the side of the defender that is away from the play.

This release is executed by simply pushing off the offensive man's near shoulder and taking an open step in the direction to be pursued. The push-off gives initial momentum and can cut pursuit time by a step or two. The open step starts the body in the proper pursuit direction and eliminates the hazardous cross-over step. This step is dangerous because it puts linemen in a position where their entire body weight is on one foot. When they are in this unbalanced position, they are vulnerable to being knocked down with the slightest contact. Eliminating the cross-over also eliminates the danger of a defensive lineman tripping over the opponent's foot or his own foot. The push-off is a basic release to get to the ball, but defensive linemen need additional techniques to get to the ball.

Spin-Out

The spin-out release is best used when the offensive man has control of the defensive man, but controls with a high block, high in the sense that the defensive man has his body weight controlled with his feet.

To a certain point the spin-out release is similar to the pass rush spin, so when you practice one technique you are developing the other. The spin-out escape is executed by first throwing the far arm (the arm away from releasing direction) around the back of the body and simultaneously twisting the head around (see Figure 7-1). The on-side foot is used as the pivot. The flailing arm will cause the leg on that side to come around (the left leg if the release is to the right). The swinging leg should be planted so that it is aimed in the direction of the pursuit. The flailing arm comes completely around and that hand is placed on the offensive man. A push off the offensive man will give the defender a good start.

The spin-out release is more effective when the defender is releasing to a play that is a few holes away from him or farther

Figure 7-1

outside. The depth of the spin is determined by the distance the defender has to go after he spins. If he has to get to the hole next to him, the cross-face release can be more effective than the spin-out.

Cross-Face

The cross-face release is a quick method of breaking an offensive block and getting to the immediate gaps to make the tackle. This technique is better than spinning because the defender never loses sight of the ball carrier. Proper execution does not require the quickness of the spins, but it does require strong biceps.

The cross-face is executed by (releasing to the left) shooting the right arm bicep through the helmet of the offensive man and attempting to get the upper part of the arm on the other side of the man's helmet (see Figure 7-2). The left arm can complement

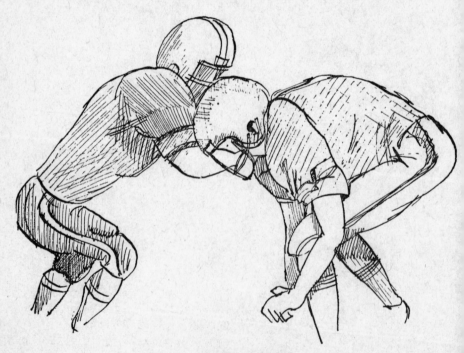

Figure 7-2

the right arm if it is brought back at the same time the right arm is brought across. When the defensive man clears the helmet of the offensive man, he is in a position to pursue the ball. If the offensive man has such control that the defender cannot use a cross-face, the seat roll will allow him to get to the ball.

Seat Roll

The seat roll allows a defender to release from a block that completely controls the defensive lineman. It is a last resort to avoid staying blocked.

The seat roll is executed by (releasing to the right) rolling the right shoulder under the body and starting a roll that is followed by the rest of the body. During the roll, the shoulders should maintain their height so that the body weight comes to rest on the seat. The roll continues by using the hands to push the seat off the ground and resting on all fours. When the seat roll is executed quickly, the seat does not rest on the ground, but merely uses the ground to push the all four position.

The seat roll can be used to release from a good angle block. This technique quickly puts a defender into an area where the blocker doesn't want him. Many times the defender will close the hole by rolling into it, even though he may not be in a ready position to make the tackle.

After your defensive lineman successfully releases from the blocker, he must take a path that will get him to the ball carrier as quickly as possible, with the ball carrier gaining as few yards as possible. The importance of the angle of pursuit is that it achieves both defensive objectives:

1. It gets the defender to the ball carrier as quickly as possible.
2. It gives the ball carrier as little gain as possible.

When the defender sets his path for the ball carrier, he must set a course to where the ball carrier will be, not where he was or is (see Figure 7-3). Defenders should always head for a point a few yards ahead of the ball. A more exact depth of the angle of pursuit is determined by the following factors:

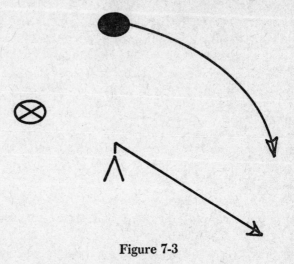

Figure 7-3

1. The speed of the ball carrier
2. The speed of the defender chasing
3. The field width in which the defender has to operate

We occasionally see backs who are so fast that they appear to outrun angles of pursuit. A few years ago we unsuccessfully defended Billy Johnson (formerly Chichester High School, pres-

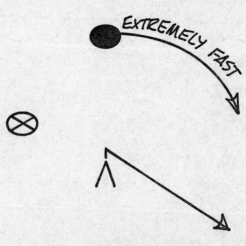

Figure 7-4

ently Houston Oilers). Billy's speed was such that when he ran outside, he would be five to ten yards ahead of the defenders who were angling after him. The point is that the defender knows where the ball carrier will ultimately be—the goal line, and he must cut him off somewhere in front of it. An exaggeration would be for the defender away from the play to run straight back for the goal line when the back starts to run wide on the 50 yard line. The faster the back, the deeper the angle of pursuit (see Figure 7-4).

A similar situation that would cause the defender to take an extra deep angle would be a lack of speed on the part of the man chasing. The greater the speed difference between the ball carrier and the chaser, the deeper the angle that the defender must take. The amount of wide side field also determines how deep the angle of pursuit will be. The farther away the sideline, the deeper the angle.

Once the defender gets set on the proper path to the ball carrier, he should maintain constant eye contact with the man with the ball. This means that he must run over and around people while looking at a moving object. The constant eye contact will allow the defender to change his path should the ball carrier cut back. While pursuing the ball carrier between the tackles, the defender should keep his hips and shoulders parallel to the line of scrimmage. Once outside the tackles, defensive linemen should run as fast as possible.

The key to getting good outside pursuit is getting started as soon as possible. Your defenders who end up near the ball carrier are the ones who get started as quickly as possible. You can substantiate this with your films by retracing the paths of your players who participate in a gang tackle.

Getting to the ball carrier is as much mental as physical. If a player believes that he can do it, he will, no matter how much a head start the ball carrier has or how many obstacles the defender has to run through. Pursuers have the advantage of knowing that the ball carrier is likely to be slowed a number of times before he is finally dropped. If the pursuer is the one being slowed, he must be prepared to meet or avoid the resistance so that he can quickly return to his normal speed.

Shedding

Shedding is the defender's technique of handling resistance that he encounters on his angle to the ball. If the defensive man can take his path to the ball without meeting any resistance, he is going to get there more quickly than if he has to have contact with players along the way. Sometimes we make our players so conscious of making contact that they go out of their way to knock someone down. The primary person we want our players to knock down is the ball carrier. That's what stops the play. If knocking someone down is not necessary, it should be avoided.

When a blocker cannot be avoided as in the case of an offensive man in the direct path of the pursuer, the defender must get rid of the blocker as efficiently and quickly as possible. An unusual delay will eliminate a pursuer from the play.

The most aggressive technique to use to clear the path to the ball carrier is similar to the offensive shoulder block. This method is good to use when the blocker is squared off and waiting for the defender. The defensive man should run through the blocker by lowering his shoulder and using the shoulder lift technique as described in Chapter 2. The defender should get as close as possible to the offensive man before he lowers his shoulder and makes contact. The key to this technique is the defensive man getting his feet practically on the toes of the offensive man. The follow-through of the shoulder shed should throw the defender to the side to keep clear the path to the tackler.

The less aggressive techniques of pursuing are quicker because there is no loss of valuable time to make contact. If the defender can take a direct path and avoid contact, he should use a less aggressive technique to avoid resistance. These techniques are variations of the spins and fakes used to rush the passer. The fake is executed by approaching the defender and taking a fake short step in one direction and pivoting off that foot and starting in a direction on the other side of the man. The other technique is to make slight contact with the blocker and spin off to one side or the other.

These latter two techniques are especially good against a

blocker who is rapidly approaching the defender. The blocker's chances of making good contact with the defender are similar to a tackler trying to stop the ball carrier when the two are headed directly for each other. The player who is trying to avoid the contact has the advantage because he has two directions in which to move. The blocker must not only react to the proper direction, but he must also make good contact with the potential tackler.

No matter how good the technique to avoid the blocker, the defender will occasionally be knocked to the ground. If your defensive man can execute a good hit-and-roll, he can quickly regain his feet and continue on his path to make the tackle.

Tackling

Releasing, pursuing, and shedding are means to an end, tackling. Practically speaking, the major objective of defense is to tackle the ball carrier. You are familiar with the emphasis of safety in tackling and the basics of tackling in most situations, but some tackling situations occur only occasionally, and they can make a direct influence on the outcome of a game. These situations are:

1. Being the last defender between the ball carrier and the goal line
2. Tackling from behind in the open field
3. Making a desperation dive

All these situations are crucial because a mistake usually results in a score.

Defensive players who aggressively pursue off-side plays will occasionally be in a position where they are the last defender between the ball and the goal line. This can easily happen when a deep back misses a tackle or is otherwise eliminated from the play. The technique to be used by the last defender is to retreat, retreat, retreat. The defender should give ground as much as possible until one of two things happens:

1. The defender can sandwich the ball carrier into the sideline.

2. The defender can slow him down until pursuit can catch up to the ball.

If neither of these situations occurs, the defender should delay the tackle until the ball carrier approaches the goal line. At this point, the tackle must be attempted. If the tackle can be made going into the sidelines, the percentages of stopping the play increase. A defensive player should use the sidelines for tackling whenever possible.

If a defender is not between the ball carrier and the goal line, he will be chasing him to the goal line. When a player is chasing the ball carrier and gaining on him, he cannot afford to miss the tackle. A missed tackle is a score. A good technique that assures an open field tackle is jumping on the back of the carrier and locking the arms around the opponent's neck and tangling the legs around his lower body. From this spider-like position, the defensive player can slide down the back's body, gradually entangling him to the ground. If he doesn't fall to the ground after that, don't worry about winning the game; try and get to know the kid so you can be his agent.

Jumping on the back is a good method of bringing down a back that a defensive player can catch, but the ones that the defense can't catch are the problems. The technique for a desperation tackle will give your defensive players an alternative other than chasing the ball carrier into the end zone. The technique is to dive for the heel of the opponent's farther back foot. The defender's extended hand should slap at the back foot in an attempt to push it forward and trip the ball carrier.

When a desperation tackle attempt isn't necessary and you can get a number of players near the ball, the secondary tacklers have two specific jobs:

1. Try to cause a fumble.
2. Insure that the ball carrier falls backwards.

You have seen the positive effect that gang tackling can have on your defense, but make sure that you get the best results from it. The effect of good pursuit should be more than a number of players making the tackle and then jumping up and down.

In conclusion the realistic objective of defense is to make the tackle. To achieve that end, defensive players must first use a quick release to get free from the blocker, take the proper angle to get to the ball carrier, and confront or avoid obstruction on the way to the ball. Certain tackling situations dictate using special techniques to make the tackle. Various stunts from different fronts offer opportunities to get to the ball carrier more quickly and to stop the play.

DRILLS

1. 3-on-1 Release.

Purpose: To develop release skills against various offensive situations.

Procedure: Defensive player faces three offensive players. Coach signals to offense for various blocking combinations. Defensive player uses one of the releases to free himself from the offensive block. The defender should release to the side of the pressure.

Comment: The correct defensive release is determined by the type of offensive block. Details are included in Chapter 7.

2. Pursuit Drill.

Purpose: To get all defensive linemen to the ball carrier.

Procedure: Defensive linemen react alternately to an inside play and an outside play (see Figure 7-5).

Comment: Every defensive lineman must be convinced that his job is important, especially a player away from the play.

3. Obstacle Course.

Purpose: To teach defensive linemen to get to the ball carrier—in spite of obstacles.

Procedure: Defensive players run through an obstacle course of offensive players and dummies to get to the ball carrier (see Figure 7-6).

Comment: Defensive player should keep his eyes on the ball carrier at all times. He should step over dummies without looking down. Shedding techniques should be used on offensive players who prevent him from remaining on his proper angle.

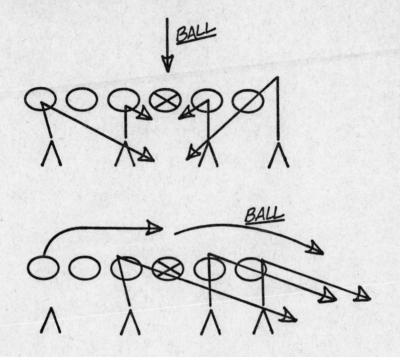

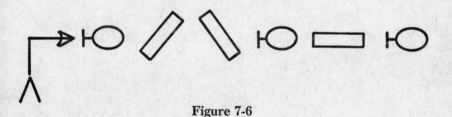

Figure 7-5

Figure 7-6

4. Body Awareness Drill.

Purpose: To develop an awareness of other players and the ability to avoid contact on the way to the ball carrier.

Procedure: Four players get in a five yard square. On a signal, they move around trying to avoid contact with another player. More players can be added to make the drill more difficult.

Comment: Do not allow players to move in a continuous circle. This drill is especially effective for players who feel that they must go out of their way to make contact. The major objective of defensive players is to stop the ball carrier and not to see how many offensive players they can knock down.

5. Shotgun Shedding Drill.

Purpose: To develop the technique of shedding an offensive player.

Procedure: Each defensive player faces a line of three offensive blockers (see Figure 7-7). Offensive players block defenders in few second intervals. Defensive players shed blockers using alternating shoulders.

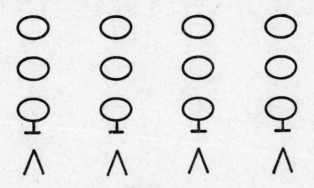

Figure 7-7

Comment: A left-right-left combination will help develop the weaker shoulders of most players. Only allow one good initial hit for each two players.

6. Blinkers Drill.

Purpose: To eliminate defensive players from blinking their eyes when they make contact tackling.

Procedure: A line of defensive players goes past a coach as he gently taps a football on the face mask of each player. Players should avoid blinking their eyes when the ball hits them.

Comment: Make "blinkers" repeat the drill. Encourage players to exaggerate, keeping their eyes open on contact.

7. Desperation Tackle Drill.

Purpose: To develop the seldom practiced technique of making a desperation tackle.

Procedure: A defender chases a ball carrier who has a lead according to his speed to the goal line (so the defender can catch him). Defensive players use either the jump-on-the-back technique or diving for the back heel.

Comment: This drill can be used as a major conditioning drill since so much running is involved.

8

Stunting Your Defense from Different Fronts

Stunting from the eight-man front. Stunting from the seven-man front. Stunting from the five-man front. Stunting from the four-man line. Playing the prevent line.

Stunting defenses offer you another method of getting your defensive linemen to the ball carrier. Stunting can be used as a change-up to your standard defense or as a basic defense itself.

Stunting does not necessarily mean gambling. Any defense is sound as long as someone is responsible for every gap. Stunting may result in some gaps being weaker than others, but it is your job to make sure that the weakest areas of the defense are the areas where the offense is least likely to run. When you stunt according to the percentages, you are making your defense stronger at the area where the offense is most likely to attack.

The amount of stunting we do is determined by our ability to control the offensive line. If our defensive linemen can consistently control the offensive line, our stunts are used only as an occasional change-up.

135

If your material is similar to ours and the asset of your defensive linemen is quickness rather than size, you also can capitalize on that speed by trying to stunt past the offensive linemen. If your defensive linemen do not have speed and do not have size either, you better add an extra digit to your scoreboard.

Stunting defenses offer a challenge to offensive linemen and test the opposing coach's blocking rules. Similar to varying alignment, stunting defenses make offensive linemen insecure. Any mental or physical hesitation on the part of the offensive linemen is a benefit to your defense.

The defense that we have successfully used is a stunting combination of the eight-man front. This type of defense is applicable to our personnel. If we ever get a group of strong linemen who can control the offensive line without stunting, we will not stunt nearly as much as we presently do.

If stunting is your philosophy, there is no limit to the number of stunts that can be designed from various fronts. Your stunts and combinations are limited only by your imagination. As you increase the number of players in your front defense, you increase the number of possible stunts and stunting combinations. Naturally, the eight-man front offers you more stunting combinations than any other standard defensive front.

Stunting from the Eight-Man Front

The eight-man defensive front is especially conducive to stunts. The linebacker on each side can execute an in and out maneuver with any of the three men in front of him (see Figure 8-1). He can also soundly cover a slant by any or all of the three on his side. When they slant, he can either go through the remaining gap or stay back in a position to cover the stunt (see Figure 8-2). You can also execute a three-on-two maneuver where the linebacker goes between any of the two defensive men (see Figure 8-3).

From the eight-man front, as well as from any of the other fronts, defensive linemen can execute a cross. Crosses can be executed by any adjacent linemen, as long as the distance be-

Figure 8-1

tween the defenders isn't too far. When your linemen cross, they exchange responsibilities. They must be aware of the job of the lineman with whom they are crossing.

Figure 8-2

Figure 8-3

There are various crossing combinations from the eight-man front (see Figure 8-4). You can also execute your linebacker stunts off the crosses (see Figure 8-5). A difficult area to cross in

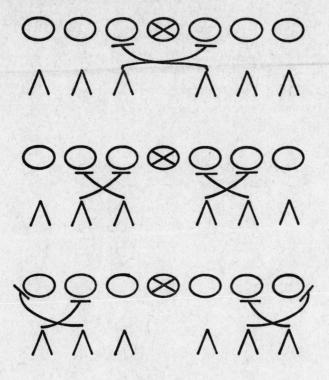

Figure 8-4

Figure 8-5

the eight-man front is the middle area. The two inside men have the offensive center between them and the distance is some-times too far to get to the responsible area. However, in a passing situation where there is a small percentage of a direct hit, the inside cross can be an effective pass-rush technique. This maneuver can also be coupled with a linebacker stunting (see Figure 8-6). An added feature of stunting your linemen from the eight-man front is that a stunt can be executed from one side, while the other side plays straight up or executes a different stunt.

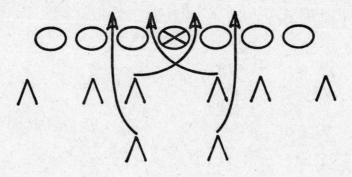

Figure 8-6

Stunting from the Seven-Man Front

The seven-man front is not very popular today as a basic defense because it has seven players in a down position and too few in an up position to pursue the football. Having seven linemen in a down position is a disadvantage against many of the wide open offenses that require defenders to be moving from sideline to sideline.

Stunts can open up a seven-man front, but the basic philosophy of the seven-man line does not encourage stunting. The principle of the seven is that each defender is better than his offensive man. If this is the case, there is little need to stunt.

However, if your seven are average or less than average, you may want to stunt to pressure the offense and give them a problem with their blocking. Basic stunts that are easily adaptable to the seven are the slants (see Figure 8-7) and crosses (see Figure 8-8). Crossing can be executed with any adjacent line-

Figure 8-7

Figure 8-8

men. The slants can be keyed to the formation, wide side, and so forth, with the linebacker (or linebackers) covering the remaining gap.

A variation of the slants is the three outside men and the nose guard slanting out with the middle backer covering inside (see Figure 8-9). A variation of the slant-out look is the linebacker and nose man executing an in and out stunt at the same time (see Figure 8-10).

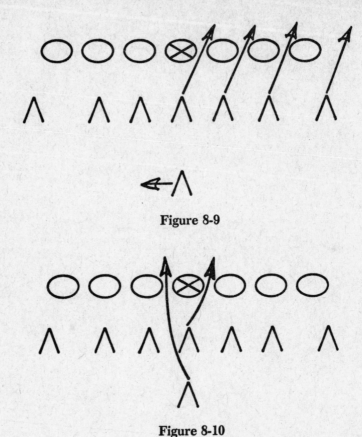

Figure 8-9

Figure 8-10

Also, the linebacker can do an in and out stunt with any inside lineman (see Figure 8-11). This is a good pass rush stunt. It can be strengthened against the run by dropping off the ends to compensate for the stunting linebacker (see Figure 8-12). Another stunt that strengthens the outside is a slant and loop stunt (see Figure 8-13). This stunt can also be executed inside (see Figure 8-14).

Stunting from the Five-Man Front

The five-man front is currently one of the most popular high school defenses. It has been somewhat successful defending the

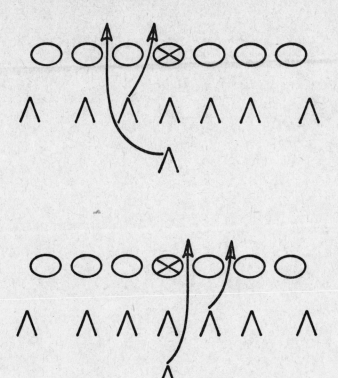

Figure 8-11

Figure 8-12

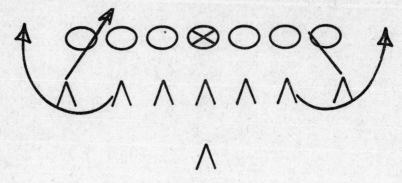

Figure 8-13

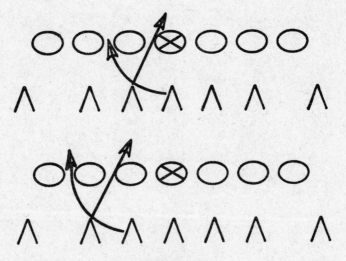

Figure 8-14

option offenses. The two linebackers make the five strong inside and the ends and corners make it strong outside.

Popular five-man stunts are the slants (see Figure 8-15) and crosses (see Figure 8-16). Linebackers can work in and out stunts with either the tackle (see Figure 8-17) or end (see Figure 8-18). Another strong off-tackle stunt from the five is the slant and loop maneuver (see Figure 8-19). Inside, the backers can stunt with the nose guard (see Figure 8-20).

Figure 8-15

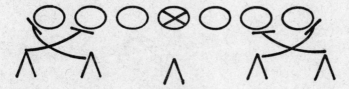

Figure 8-16

Figure 8-17

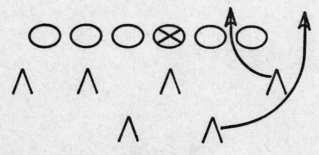

Figure 8-18

Figure 8-19

Figure 8-20

Stunting from the Four-Man Line

This popular pro-style defense is predicated on the idea that four down defensive linemen can control the six offensive linemen. The three backers are available to help with the pass or run. The three linebackers can also stunt with the front four.

The crosses are relatively safe in this defense because the backers are close by to cover. The inside men can cross with each other (see Figure 8-21) or with the outside men (see Figure 8-22). The middle backer can work an in and out maneuver with either of the inside men (see Figure 8-23). The outside backers can execute an in and out with the outside linemen or they can go between the linemen on the split end side (see Figure 8-24). The standard slants can be done in the normal way with the backers filling the gaps away from the slant (see Figure 8-25).

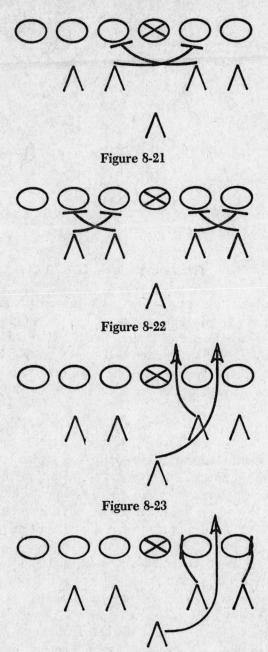

Figure 8-21

Figure 8-22

Figure 8-23

Figure 8-24

Figure 8-25

Playing the Prevent Line

All athletes like challenges and a prevent defense offers your defensive linemen a challenge offered in no other part of the game. Three defensive linemen are given the task of getting past six or seven offensive men and sometimes two additional backfield blockers. Despite these odds, we frequently see one of those three prevent defenders make a sack at a time that is always crucial.

Prevent linemen have either an inside or outside pass rush responsibility, but they have a lot of freedom within those limits. The middle man has no other responsibility than rushing the passer from the inside. He even has help with the draw.

The outside men have outside rush responsibility, but the passer is not likely to run because time and distance are usually against him. His unlikeliness to run is an advantage to the outside rusher.

All three linemen should use the definite pass situation to their advantage by getting up on the ball and trying to get the jump on the offensive men who are going back to set up to pass block. The prevent linemen face a three-on-one or two-on-one, but the situation can be used in their favor because offensive linemen are likely to let down when another person is sharing the responsibility with them. Offensive linemen frequently expect the other lineman to take the initiative and consequently neither one of them frequently blocks his best.

Another defensive advantage is that the prevent linemen have their choice of gaps to use to get into the backfield. This gives them a wider area to execute their pass rushing skills. Also, the wider area keeps offensive linemen unsure of the intended rush lane of the defender.

In conclusion, stunting can be an effective method of making a good defensive line better. Stunts can often be the equalizer that a quick line needs to match a strong line. An actively moving defensive line can pose additional problems for the offense for which they may not be prepared to defend.

Stunting can help a defensive line beat an offensive line, but additional skills are necessary to beat specific offenses. Those specific maneuvers are discussed in Chapter 9.

DRILLS

1. Musical Defenses.

Purpose: To teach alignment of various defenses.

Procedure: Your defensive line aligns on the ball. The coach takes the position of the offensive center (see Figure 8-26). The coach calls out a defense and quickly snaps the ball. The defensive linemen move to their designated areas on the snap.

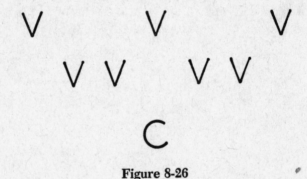

Figure 8-26

Comment: When the defenses are well known, they can be changed a number of times before the ball is snapped. The better the defenses are known, the quicker they can be changed.

2. Musical Stunts.

Purpose: To teach alignment and execution of defensive stunts.

Procedure: Use the same procedure as musical defenses.

Comment: Stunting defenses frequently require players to know a number of maneuvers in addition to their defensive assignments. The stunts must be taught similarly to the defenses.

3. Individual Stunts.

Purpose: To teach the fine points of your individual stunts.

Prodedure: Execute each one of your stunts individually with only the players involved. Figure 8-27 shows an example of an in and out maneuver with a lineman and linebacker. You must stress the individual coaching points of each stunt.

Figure 8-27

Comment: When we use an in and out maneuver, we want to put pressure on one offensive man. We want our down linemen to make contact with a shoulder to occupy the offensive man and possibly turn his shoulder so the linebacker can get past him. Coaching points similar to these should be emphasized on each stunt.

9

Adjusting Defensive Linemen to Specific Offenses

Attacking option offenses. Defending the Wing-T. Playing against the Pro. Breaking the wedge. Defending the goal line.

Before you specifically defend any offense, you must know generally what you have to defend. You have to know what your opponents like to do best and what they like to do least. Your scouting report must give you the following tendencies:

1. Formation
2. Down and distance
3. Hash mark
4. Field position

You must also know their favorite running play, inside and out-side, as well as their favorite pass, long and short. After you know generally what your opponent likes to do, you must learn the specific strengths and weaknesses of what they do.

A general knowledge of what they like to do includes a thorough knowledge of the opposing coach. The coach's personality can reveal much information about his game plan. A coach with a stubborn personality is likely to be determined to run what his team runs best. He will convince his players that his team can run a certain play and he is determined to run it—no matter how many times you stop it. This type of coach is unlikely to deviate from his basic game plan.

You can scout your opposing coach by analyzing what he has done in past games against you. Did he follow his basic game plan? Did he surprise you with something he hadn't shown previously? Was he patient? When things went wrong, did he go for the big play?

If you want to prepare yourself for your opposing coach's innovations, find out which clinics he went to during the off season. When you happen to be attending the same clinics, be sure to take notes when someone is speaking about your opponent's offense.

Many coaches have a tendency to run part of the basic offense of a close friend. This gives you an added opportunity to find out your opponent's offense. All this information can be helpful when you plan your defense for a specific offense and a specific coach.

Attacking Option Offenses

As previously mentioned, before you design a defense for an offense, you must know the strengths and weaknesses of that offense. Option offenses, the Wishbone, Veer, and some other variations are predicated on the dive play. This is the play that they first try to make go. When they can successfully run this play, the plays that they run off the dive are that much more difficult to defend. Once the dive play is established, the option offenses like to get outside with the quarterback and then with the pitch back.

All of these options cause a vulnerable situation at the point where the options are made. Those critical points are:

1. The dive hand off and read between the quarterback and the dive back (see Figure 9-1)

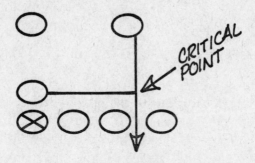

Figure 9-1

2. The quarterback's decision to keep or pitch and his pitching the ball (see Figure 9-2)

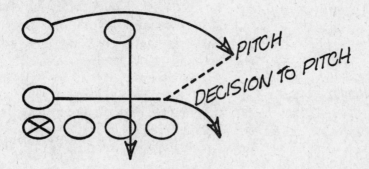

Figure 9-2

3. The pitch back catching the ball

The job of the offensive line is to make these situations as safe as possible.

In most situations the option decision is based on the position of the defensive linemen. The offensive linemen try to put the defensive linemen in a position where they are least likely to stop the play.

To attack option offenses and beat the linemen who are protecting for it, you have a number of defensive options:

1. Stunt.
2. Play strength on strength.
3. Play tendencies.
4. Play man for man.
5. Play the wide side of the field.

Since the critical points of the option are based on reads, those reads should be made as difficult as possible. Do not give the offense the security of reading the same defensive men in the same positions, play after play.

Varying alignment (Chapter 1) can make the reading difficult as can executing an in and out stunt with the linebacker and linemen who are being read. A slant can also be used effectively. The key to making the read as difficult as possible is variety with your defensive attack.

You can get a lot of variety through stunting. Inside and outside stunts will make the reads and blocks difficult because offensive linemen will be blocking different players. If you are playing the option man for man, the stunts can involve the switching of assignments of the men assigned to the dive back, quarterback, and pitch back.

Another approach to attacking the option is to correlate the strength of the offense with the strength of your defense. In other words, play your best defenders against what your opponent does best.

Another method of playing the strength of the offense is strengthening your defense to the wide side of the field. Since the offense will not have as much field to run to the short side, you need not defend this side as you would the wide side.

Regardless of which philosophy you use to attack the option, your success will be determined by how well your linemen play one-on-one. Your stunts may give you an open man in the backfield and playing tendencies may put your best men where the play is being run, but your defensive linemen must read the play and stop it.

The ideal way to stop the option is to beat the offensive linemen one-on-one. Of course, if your defensive linemen can beat their opponents head-up, you are going to beat any offense. Realistically, your linemen are going to have to know how to read and react to the actions of the option linemen. Occasionally, one of your linemen is going to beat his man by playing head-up, using a stunt, or playing a tendency. But to be consistent, your linemen are going to have to read and react on every play.

The key type of block that they are going to have to react to is the reach block. Beating the reach block will get them into the gap where the dive is being run and in the outside path where the quarterback will run.

The reach block is read by reading the head of the offensive linemen. When the offensive man is going to reach, his head will come off the line low and hard in an attempt to get position between the defensive man and where the dive back is running. When your defensive lineman reads the direction of his man's helmet, he must use the cross-face technique (described in Chapter 7) and get his bicep across his opponent's head and into the gap that the offensive man is trying to seal off. Once your lineman gets his arm across, he should take an open step to that side to get his body in position to make the hit on the dive back.

Some of the zone blocking rules for the option require that the offensive lineman take a parallel step before going to his assigned man or area. When the defensive lineman reads that zone step, he should mirror that step of the offensive man.

The most difficult block for your lineman to read and react to is the head-on block. This block usually indicates that the diveback is coming directly behind that block. This is the time that the defender must play a strong head-up technique. The shoulder lift will most likely be your defender's strongest initial charge. He must execute the technique so that he can play the area on either side of the offensive man. The least you must expect from your lineman in this situation is a stalemate. A stalemate will keep the hole as small as possible.

If your defensive man can drive his man into the backfield, you can cause a severe problem to the option quarterback. The penetration will cause a hump which the quarterback has to run around (see Figure 9-3). If this hump is at the mesh point between the quarterback and the dive back, you can possibly cause a fumble at the point of exchange.

Figure 9-3

After your lineman successfully makes the read and gets a position to take the dive back, you have a choice of philosophies as to how your lineman plays the dive back. Your lineman can take him man-for-man with the idea that the dive back knows that he is going to be taken on every play whether he has the ball or not. The other philosophy is for the defensive lineman to play the dive back with his inside shoulder, leaving the outside shoulder free to pursue the option to the outside.

We prefer to play the diveback man-for-man. We don't want to give our lineman an option for not taking the dive back. This method cuts down on some pursuit, but it assures us that someone is taking the dive back on every play.

The choice of philosophies is also applicable to playing the quarterback. When he is played man for man, he will know that he is being hit on every play, and he may tend to make the pitch with caution. Another method is to play him like he is running a sweep. As long as he has the ball, the man assigned to him takes him; when a pitch is made, the man assigned him takes a deep angle to cut off the pitch man (see Figure 9-4). We prefer to play the quarterback man for man so that he comes out on the option

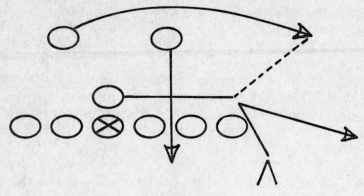

Figure 9-4

knowing that he is going to get hit, whether he keeps or pitches. Also, it reduces the mental responsibility of the man assigned to the quarterback.

The option is one of the most difficult offenses that we have to defend. Currently, defenses have not caught up to stopping it. Our best defense currently is to use a variety of techniques and to use most often the techniques that work most effectively.

Defending the Wing-T

Another type of offense that is currently popular among high schools, particularly in the Eastern states near Delaware, is the Wing-T. The high schools in this area are very likely to see this offense at least once during a season. Facing any offense only once during a season makes it very difficult to defend. But with some offenses, seeing them only once a season is once too often.

Playing against the Wing-T only once a season is difficult because your defensive linemen will be subjected to numerous offensive line skills that they will not be used to seeing.

Wing-T line play involves numerous traps (inside and outside), cross blocks, and double teams. In addition, the backfield option includes a lot of misdirection, ball handling, and isolation on defensive linemen.

Playing against all the movement of the Wing-T requires much concentration and discipline of the basic defensive skills. The most important skill to use against this type of offense is to read the offensive men in the area. These linemen will provide the keys to plays such as: traps, counters, reverses, and powers. Since power plays with double team blocking at the point of attack are common to this offense, you should prepare your defensive linemen with techniques for defeating the double team (Chapter 3).

Another key to Wing-T plays is pulling linemen, particularly guards. Generally, pulling linemen are the key to this offense. A valuable finding in your scouting report is whether or not your opponent uses a sucker trap play (see Figure 9-5) and pulls a lineman away from the point of attack. Be sure that you don't confuse this play with an offensive lineman blowing an assignment and pulling in the wrong direction.

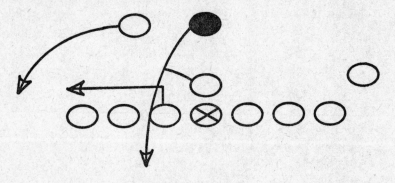

Figure 9-5

To defend these pulls that key the play, your defensive linemen should mirror the pulling offensive linemen. You should also devote equal time to defend against being trapped. Many different kinds of traps are characteristic of the Wing-T offense. In addition to guards trapping, tackles, ends, and wingbacks also trap.

All the intricate Wing-T line play requires is good timing on the part of the offensive linemen. The easiest way to upset that timing is to get someone into the offensive backfield. Penetration usually causes problems to the Wing-T offense. Consequently, you should try stunting your defensive linemen to get one of them into the offensive backfield.

While penetration causes a problem, over-penetration does not cause a problem because the defender usually takes himself out of the play. If he over-penetrates when he is being trapped, he doesn't even have to be blocked.

When the defender correctly gets one yard into the backfield, his problems are just beginning. The many backs involved in handling the ball make it difficult for your linemen to discern exactly who has the ball. If your lineman loses sight of the ball, he should hold his ground and tackle any back who comes near him. If he doesn't tackle the ball carrier, he will often get the back who is intended to get the ball.

Playing against the Wing-T will be a good test for your defensive linemen. If they can play well against this type of offense, they should do well against most offenses that you face.

Playing Against the Pro

The Pro offense is predicated on a strong passing attack. With the threat of a pass so common, you can also expect the screen and draw. The passing attack is usually complemented by such running plays as: dives, traps, sweeps, quick pitches, and the power off tackle.

The primary skill of the offensive linemen in the Pro type of attack is the pass block. This means that defensively you must refine your pass rushing techniques and your rushing the passer skills. These techniques should always be practiced along with defending the screen and draw.

The wide line splits that are characteristic of the Pro allow you to stunt to get additional pressure on the passer. The stunts may also prove effective against the run. Penetration can usually cause a problem to the quick hitting plays of a Pro offense.

When you are not stunting, you can key the plays of the Pro by having your linemen read the offensive linemen in their area. Offensive linemen still key plays like: dives, traps, sweeps, and the power off tackle.

Breaking the Wedge

The wedge attack is frequently used as a short yardage attack. It is designed to gain only a few yards. All the offensive linemen block toward the point of the wedge while the back with the ball patiently follows the slow developing offensive blocking. The wedge, like a chain, is weakest at its weakest point. When a defensive lineman penetrates the point of the wedge, it is broken.

We have found success in breaking the wedge by using a goal-line charge to penetrate it. When we haven't been able to penetrate it, we have stopped it by stopping the progress of the offensive linemen. When they can't move, the back behind them can't move.

Defending the Goal Line

When your opponent makes a first down inside the ten yard line, your defensive line must prepare to show its character. Your defense is in a position where it cannot stretch any farther and you are protecting the last few feet you have before your opponent might score.

In goal line situations, mental preparation is as important as physical preparation. You, as the coach, should be prepared mentally by making sure that your best linemen are on the field. If you are a two-platoon team, you may want to use a few linemen from the offense. These types of substitutions are easy if you use more down linemen on your goal line defense than you use on your normal defense.

Regardless of whom you are using, the goal line defense has to start getting ready when the offense comes out of the huddle. If the offense is in the huddle longer than usual, you should expect something other than the usual goal line plays. As your opponent breaks the huddle, your defensive linemen should literally dig in. They want to be sure to have good traction so they can get a quick, strong charge.

Your linemen must be ready to come off the ball a little quicker than usual. Most teams like to use a quick count off the goal line so that they reduce the chance of the offensive line going off-sides.

Your defensive line must also be prepared for the silent count quarterback sneak. Defending this play requires your middle men to concentrate on the ball. If they don't move on the first movement of the ball, they will not stop the sneak.

Also to protect against the sneak, you must give someone the responsibility of stopping the progress of the center. If the center can't move forward, the quarterback will not be able to move forward. If you play an even goal line defense, the two inside men can stop the sneak by making contact with the center on each thigh. This assignment is much more difficult for one defensive lineman who is playing head-up.

There are two "musts" for your defensive linemen when they are in a goal line situation:

1. They must get off the ball quickly.
2. They must penetrate into the offensive backfield.

To accomplish both these objectives, the defensive linemen must be up on the ball. If you constantly play your defense off the ball to stunt, vary alignment, or for some other reason, they must be sure to be up tight on the goal line.

To get off the ball quickly, defensive linemen must move on movement (Chapter 1). Quick movement is necessary to penetrate the offensive backfield—a must on the goal line. As mentioned in Chapter 2, the key to getting through on the goal line charge is the twisting action of the shoulders to get through the offensive linemen.

Once into the offensive backfield, defensive linemen must make the tackle by making a direct hit, a little higher than usual. The purpose of the higher hit is to make the ball carrier fall backwards. A six foot tall back who falls forward will gain two yards. Two yards is two too many on the goal line.

Stopping the progress of the ball is more important than stopping the progress of the back. You want to keep the ball out of the end zone. If your linemen can only stop the progress of the ball carrier, your linebackers must insure that the ball carrier falls backwards.

Stopping the opponent on the goal line gives a psychological advantage to the defense by making them believe that the offense cannot score. You, the coach, are not as elated because you know that your offense must get the ball out of a dangerous area.

In conclusion, playing against different types of offenses requires slight adjustments to your defensive line play. The basics of defensive line play remain the same, but variations are necessary to defend what your linemen are not used to seeing from week to week.

The best key that you have against any offense is reading the offensive linemen in the area. This is common to all offenses. When you are prepared for the specifics of your opponent's offense, you are ready for whatever they have to offer. Occasionally, your opponent will offer you the ball. Chapter 10 will discuss techniques of "scooping and scoring."

DRILLS

1. Play Recognition Drill.

Purpose: To expose defensive linemen to opponent's offensive plays.

Procedure: Defensive linemen stand at their positions. They watch an offensive team first walk through the opponent's predominant plays and then watch them run through those plays.

Comment: This drill is the initial step in the progression of teaching defensive reactions to offensive keys. After they see the complete play, they can be drilled to react to their individual keys.

2. Pride Drill.

Purpose: To develop pride in preventing points on the goal line.

Procedure: An offensive team gets four plays to score from the four. The defense prevents them from scoring.

Comment: The purpose of the drill is to develop pride in the goal line defense. To achieve this, select your offensive players accordingly. If your goal line defense cannot match your offense, you should not use this type of drill.

10

Capitalizing on Fumbles

Causing fumbles. Recovering fumbles. "Scooping and scoring."

Knowing the idiosyncracies of the different offenses will be an asset when you have to stop them, but sometimes there is an easier way to get the ball back—cause a fumble. Many of us are constantly instructing our defense to get the ball back, but few of us actually teach the techniques to cause a fumble, recover it and "scoop and score." If we only preach it and neglect to teach it, our defense isn't likely to do it.

When the defense starts to cause fumbles, recover them and advance them; players will react to a loose ball like it belongs to them. They will not be surprised to see a fumbled ball, and they will expect to recover it when they see it. And what greater sight is there than seeing a tackle score?

The first step in your lineman's materialization of his vision of grandeur is to cause the fumble. An attempt to cause a fumble begins with an analysis of the way a ball is held by the ball carrier. The most protected parts of the ball are the two sides.

One side is protected by the ball carrier's forearm and the other side is fortified further with his body. It is unlikely that a fumble will be caused by attacking the ball from the outside, and it is almost impossible to attack the ball from the inside.

The top and bottom of the ball are not in contact with any part of the body and are completely exposed. The front point of the ball is protected with the hand and the back point is completely vulnerable. In studying a correctly held football, we find that the most unprotected areas of the ball are the top and bottom and the rear point. If we are going to cause fumbles, these are the areas to attack.

Causing Fumbles

Knowing what to attack to cause a fumble, the problem remains of how to attack. The method of attacking the vulnerable areas of the ball is determined by the angle at which the defensive player is making the tackle. Some tackling angles are more conducive to causing fumbles than other angles.

Blind side tackles on the ball side cause more fumbles than any other type of hit. Prior to a routine tackle, the ball carrier prepares himself for the hit by tightening his muscles, causing him to tighten his grip on the ball. When the hit is unexpected, the ball grip is not as secure, and he is more likely to lose control of the ball.

Your defensive linemen must take advantage of the weaker grip and aggressively attack the ball when they can make a hit unexpected to the ball carrier. If the surprise hit comes from the side, the defender should attack the ball from the top down. The common technique is to hammer the fist down through the ball. This method does not jeopardize the tackle because the shoulder will immediately follow the hand through the ball and through the ball carrier's midsection. The opposite hand is also available to grasp a leg.

The most likely opportunity to cause a fumble is caused by a tackle from the direct rear. The hit is unexpected and the most vulnerable part of the ball is exposed—the rear point. The fumble is caused by the defender getting a hand in the rear space between the back point of the ball and the ball carrier's elbow (see Figure 10-1). A defender's hand in this location can act as a wedge and force the ball down. The wedge technique is further enhanced by the hit being unexpected.

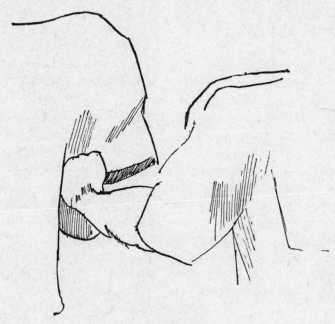

Figure 10-1

The wedge technique is the method to use when you are losing in the last few minutes and you need the ball back. Even when the offense is expecting the ball to be knocked out, the back point is frequently exposed. As soon as a defender can get a hand in this area, the ball is likely to come out. Getting the ball loose is half the way of getting the ball back; the other half is recovering it.

Recovering Fumbles

When your opponent mishandles the ball, you have an easy opportunity to stop their drive—provided you can recover the loose ball. We have been successful at causing and recovering fumbles by using the four "R" method:

1. Rake
2. Recognize
3. React
4. Recover

Players must be conditioned to react to a loose ball as if they expected it and not as though they are surprised by it. When the ball is loose, the defense has just as much right to it as the offense does. Your players must believe that, and you must incorporate that thinking into your practice.

Your players react to the ball by either seeing it or being alerted to it. Many teams draw attention to the ball by yelling "ball." This word does alert players to a loose ball—but it alerts twenty-two players and not just your eleven players. Why give the offense equal opportunity? The idea of alerting only the defense to the ball was initiated by our secondary coach, Mike Lashendock. He convinced us to use a word that only our team was conditioned to and not the opponent. Now, we not only have the advantage of recovering fumbles that we recognize, but we also have the advantage of being alerted to our opponent's fumbles when they yell "ball." Most of our opponents believe in equal opportunity.

The successful recovery of a fumble depends on quick reaction. Recovering a fumble is easy when your opponent doesn't see it. But when both teams recognize the ball, the players who use the better techniques are going to recover it.

The technique to recover a loose ball in a congested area is to get the hips lower than the person who is challenging you to the ball. The principle is the same as the one-on-one—whoever gets lower gets the ball. Getting the hips lower is crucial because in this position, the opponent will automatically be pushed aside when going after a loose ball. When the hips are on the same level, the stronger player is going to get the ball. When one player has his hips lower, he has the better chance to get the ball.

When the hips are lower, the trunk will be lower and the player will have a direct shot at the ball—but that doesn't mean that he will get the ball. Many high school fumbles are lost by a player diving directly at the ball and causing it to bounce away in an unpredictable direction.

The technique the lower lineman should use is grabbing the ball with extended hands and rolling a shoulder over the ball. The shoulder should roll into the opposition. This will screen the opponents from having a clean shot at the ball. In essence, the defender can screen the opposition with one shoulder and scoop the ball with the other arm.

The scoop method can also be used when the defender is on the ground. Either arm can be used to scoop the ball. To use this technique while on the ground, the head should be raised so that the ball does not bounce off the helmet.

With all types of ground fumble recoveries, the ball must be brought into the body and protected. The body should curl around the ball and the ball should be further protected with the arms and legs.

While the ball is protected, players who do not recover the ball should protect the player who gets the ball. At the same time the other players should expect to recover another fumble, should the ball be loose again. Defensive linemen get a lot of pleasure from recovering a loose ball, but not half the pleasure you'll both get from "scooping and scoring."

"Scooping and Scoring"

Our philosophy on fumbles has been to pick up the ball and run with it. During a recent season we had one fumble returned for a 95 yard touchdown, another returned for a 60 yard score, and a tackle caught from behind after running 40 yards. We encourage "scooping and scoring" on almost every fumble. When we initiated the philosophy of running with a loose ball, we were concerned that our players would be scooping when they should be diving and that we would be losing some fumbles that we should have been recovering. But it didn't happen that way. Players seem to have a natural instinct that causes them to dive for balls when there is congestion and when the situation is critical. Consequently, we always preach "scooping and scoring."

To teach this technique, you must practice the different ways that a loose ball can be encountered:

1. The ball can be coming directly to the player (see Figure 10-2.)
2. The ball can be moving away from the player (see Figure 10-3)
3. The ball can be motionless as the player approaches.

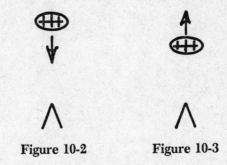

Figure 10-2   Figure 10-3

The technique for picking up the ball in each situation is slightly different.

The Ball Coming to the Player

This is the most difficult method of the three because if the player misses the ball, it will usually go past him. The player should approach the ball in a crouched position with the hands dangling low at the sides. The palms should be open and a few inches outside each foot (see Figure 10-4). This approach position gives a snowplow effect that extends about three feet across. This range is necessary to protect an unpredictable bounce. If that occurs, the ball can be plowed back in the direction in which the defender is going.

By approaching the ball with the palms up, the defender has his hands in position not only to keep the ball in front of him

Figure 10-4

should it take a weird bounce, but also to get another try to pick it up. He should pick it up with his dominant hand by getting that palm under the bottom of the ball and scooping it up into the other hand. The momentum of the ball coming up will make it easy to clamp.

Many defensive linemen in their haste to pick up the ball, accidentally kick it forward as they bend to get it. This is usually done with the foot on the side of the hand with which they are scooping. Ideally, they should reach down off the foot opposite the hand they are using to scoop. This technique is a difficult skill and you should work on it if your linemen are having a problem kicking the ball.

The Ball Moving Away from the Player

A defensive lineman frequently faces a ball in this situation after a blocked punt, a fumble in the backfield or a blind side hit on the passer. The ball is moving toward your goal line and your lineman sees the ball, the goal line, a clear field and his opportunity for infamy. Picking up the ball seems simple, but boys will be boys.

Your defensive lineman will be relaxed in this situation if he can concentrate on making the recovery step-by-step. When he is pursuing the ball moving away from him, he should first stop the roll of the ball. If he can concentrate on this step first, he will not have time to imagine himself scoring. The roll of the ball should be stopped similarly to a catcher fielding bunts. He should reach past the ball with the palm of one hand and scoop the ball with the other. The pickup scoop is the same as the technique for scooping a ball that is moving into a defender. The approach to the ball should be slightly to the side of the ball rather than head-on. The side approach reduces the chances of the ball being kicked.

The Ball Motionless as the Player Approaches

The method of approaching a motionless ball is similar to approaching a ball that is moving away from the defender. The motionless ball is more often mishandled by being over-run.

The technique to avoid over-running the ball is to reach for the ball, first with the palm under the near side of the ball, and then with the other hand over the other side to stop the forward motion caused by the first hand. Similar to the other techniques, the ball should be approached from the side. When a motionless ball is picked up or any other loose ball is recovered, the ball should be hooked into the stomach and tucked away. We frequently overlook teaching defensive linemen to put the ball away and run, but there are two good reasons for teaching it. The most obvious reason is that defensive linemen are likely to recover a fumble at some time during their career and they should know what to do with it. They can very easily be taught to zig-zag with the ball to avoid a tackler. This simple maneuver makes a pursuer's tackle a little more difficult, and it may result in a score.

The other reason to teach running with the football is psychological. If a defensive lineman imagines himself scoring and he practices scoring, he will become conditioned to thinking about scoring. When he gets an opportunity to "scoop and score," he will already have experienced the success of the play.

We practice success by running a drill that gives every defensive player the experience of picking up a fumble, running for a touchdown, handing the ball to the official, doing a "TD dance," and being mobbed by the rest of the defense. This may sound romanticized, but when our defensive linemen score, they do the same procedure in the game that they do in practice.

Developing techniques for recovering fumbles is a small point that often results in six points. As you develop additional small points, you increase your chances of getting a big win.

DRILLS

1. Gauntlet Drill.

Purpose: To develop the skill of causing fumbles.

Procedure: Defensive players form two parallel rows as ball carrier runs between them. Defensive players try to cause a fumble by using the techniques described in Chapter 10.

Comment: This drill is frequently used as an offensive drill, but it also can be used as a defensive drill.

2. Two on the Ball.

Purpose: To develop the reactions and skills to recover fumbles.

Procedure: A coach throws the ball between two defensive players who try to recover it.

Comment: Throw the ball a different way every time to condition them to the unpredictable bounces of the ball.

3. Grab It.

Purpose: To develop the reactions for a fumble recovery and the ability to take the ball from another player.

Procedure: Two players face each other on all fours with their helmets touching. A ball is placed between them. Their hands are placed flat on the ground behind the ball. When the coach removes his hand from the top of the ball, the players try to grab the ball.

Comment: We use this drill as a fun-type drill. We separate winners from losers and run an elimination to get the quickest hands on the team.

4. Fielding Fumbles.

Purpose: To develop the skills of fielding fumbles three different ways: coming, going, and motionless.

Procedure: A coach throws fumbles to be fielded the three different ways.

Comment: When we run this drill, we like to emphasize how few misses we have.

5. TD Drill.

Purpose: To give defensive players the feeling of picking up a fumble, scoring, handing the ball to the official, and being mobbed by the remainder of the defense.

Procedure: The above situation is simulated.

Comment: This drill conditions players to think about scoring.

11

Use Little Things
to Get a Big
Defensive Advantage

*Adjusting to wide splits. Adjusting to junk offenses.
Preparing for PATs. Changing to offense. Adjusting
to fourth down. Facing field goals. Reading audibles.
Playing two-minute defense. Psychological approaches
to defensive linemen. Agility.*

You must prepare in a special way for each different offense
that you face each week, but some segments of defensive line
play never change. They are the little things that you must
practice during the week, and they very often make a big difference on game day.

The little things are only important when you have to use
them. If some of these situations never occur, you have lost only
practice time, but you have the satisfaction of knowing that your
linemen are ready for almost any situation.

In preparing for the little things, we should not neglect to prepare our defense for any unusual offense that is part of our own attack. We use an unusual spread formation for our two-point conversion. After using it for five games during an undefeated season, we were embarrassed when our opponent suddenly ran "our" spread against us. We won the game and also won a valuable lesson in preparation. We now prepare against every unusual play and formation that is part of our offense. This also includes defending a cross-pass that is part of our kick return offense.

Your coaching experience will tell you what additional situations you should prepare against. Some extremely unusual situations may cost you a game, but don't let them cost you a lesson.

Adjusting to Wide Splits

Occasionally, an offensive play or formation may attempt to stretch your defense by using extremely wide splits. The offensive philosophy, and a good one, is to try to create a natural hole by stretching the defense with the offense. If the defense doesn't stretch, the offense tries to take advantage of unusual blocking angles.

When your linemen are faced with this situation, they should remember that they should always be in a position to perform their responsibilities. Obviously, a defensive lineman cannot perform his job if he is a yard outside his normal alignment or if he is giving up an easy downblock.

A common method to defend against wide splits is defensive men moving half way between the two offensive linemen and then moving off the ball about a yard and a half to two yards (see Figure 11-1), depending on the size of the split.

Your linemen can create more of a problem by first lining up on one of the offensive men, waiting until an offensive call is made, and then moving to the final position. If you want a more aggressive way to defend the wide splits, you can stunt through the extremely wide split in an attempt to get quickly into the backfield. If the stunt is successful, you should continue to use it.

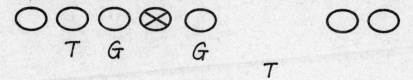

Figure 11-1

Adjusting to Junk Offenses

An extension of extremely wide splits is a junk formation play or a junk formation offense. If your opponent has shown this offense in previous games, you will have no problem being prepared. The problem occurs when your opponent surprises you with something unusual.

To defend against this you must be prepared with some general guidelines that can cover almost any unusual situation. The first instinct of our defensive captain when confronted with an unusual situation is to call time out. Before doing this however, the captain must be aware of the number of time outs remaining and how crucial they are to the outcome of the game.

We instruct our defensive captain to call time out anytime he wishes in the first half, especially if the offense does something for which we are unprepared. In the second half, all time outs are called from the bench.

With these instructions, the defensive captain must be prepared to make the adjustments for unusual offensive formations. When our defensive captain makes the call "junk," we automatically turn to the following responsibilities:

1. Our two inside linemen charge from both sides of the center (see Figure 11-2). If the center has no other linemen near him, the guards pressure the play from both sides of the center.

2. Our outside men, the ones who have outside responsibility, line up in a position where they can defend the outside (see Figure 11-3). If the offensive formation is extremely spread, the ends usually have to move back off the ball.

3. All other defensive linemen line up where the strength of the offensive line is located.

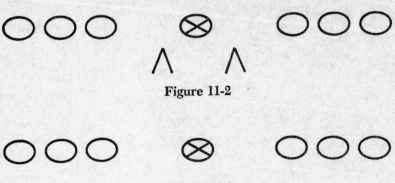

Figure 11-2

Figure 11-3

In essence, our "junk" assignments are to pressure the ball from the inside, defend the corners, and meet strength with strength.

Preparing for PATs

Your first preparation for touchdown conversions must be mental because your defense will be down after having been scored upon. You must impress upon your defense the value of avoiding extra points and how many games are decided by the extra point margin.

Nobody likes to be scored upon, but six points isn't as bad as seven, and seven isn't as bad as eight. To emphasize the value of these few points, review the scores of the previous season. Point out how often both teams score the same number of touchdowns and how many games were decided by the extra points.

After being mentally prepared, you must have prepared a conversion defense that takes care of the following:

1. Defends a pass or run attempt for two points
2. Blocks a kick attempt
3. Defends a fake kick attempt for two points

Your first defensive concern on PATs should be to avoid two

points. This is a situation for your standard defenses, but alter them with the following considerations:

1. Someone or something failed somewhere or you wouldn't be in the extra point situation.
2. More two point plays are run outside than inside.
3. Many teams prefer pass/run option type plays for two-point conversions.
4. A quarterback has no fear of being intercepted on a conversion attempt.
5. When the offensive team is in the huddle, you don't know if you need a defense for a pass/run, block, or fake kick.

If your opponent lines up for a kick, you should be prepared with a block that exploits a weakness that you scouted. Your kick block may be influenced by one of the following factors:

1. A center whose block is weakened because he fails to bring his head up to block
2. The weakest offensive lineman
3. A lineman who fails to turn to the inside when that particular kind of blocking is used
4. A lineman who doesn't tighten his split

When you design your block, be sure that the center always has someone on his head so that he will be conscious of contact whenever he makes a long snap with his head down. Be sure that you don't overburden your defensive players with too many kick blocks. In addition to the mental strain, you are assuming that your opponent will score a number of times.

Changing to Offense

If your players have confidence in their offense, a turnover will come as no surprise to them. They will not be thrilled with merely getting the ball; they will expect to gain some yardage and score. You will be capitalizing on your opponent's psychological letdown of just having lost possession of the ball.

Your defense should be alerted to the quick change with an alerting call. As mentioned previously, don't use a term that also alerts the offensive team. When the call is made, the defense should immediately look for an opponent to block. Some teams use set return plays on a turnover, but we prefer to have our ball carrier run for daylight. Regardless of how you return the ball, blocks must be picked up immediately. Many inexperienced players prefer to do more looking than blocking.

The only opponent that should be looked for is the intended receiver or the person who has just lost the ball. After him, opponents closest to the ball carrier should be blocked first.

Adjusting to Fourth Down

Fourth down offers you almost as many variations as a touchdown conversion. You must be prepared for fourth down with a defense that offers many alternatives. You must be prepared with defenses that allow you to do one of the following:

1. Defend a normal pass or run
2. Block a kick
3. Return a kick
4. Defend a fake from punt formation

The defense that you have on the field must be prepared to do all of these things. If you use a specialty team, they must be prepared to do all of them.

When your opponent aligns in a normal formation on fourth down, you must be prepared to defend the following:

1. A pass or run
2. A shift into punt formation
3. A quick kick

If your opponent lines up in punt formation, your first assumption must be that they are going to fake the punt. This assumption will always keep you conscious of the fake. You must expect the fake to develop in a number of ways:

1. A trick play such as a screen or reverse
2. A pass or run
3. A snap to one of the short backs

All these fake options necessitate your being in a sound fourth down defense.

To avoid being surprised on fourth down, you should look for one of the following keys:

1. A different player in punt formation
2. A longer time in the huddle
3. The center looking to the side to snap to someone other than the punter
4. A variation in the punt formation alignment, such as the punter being closer or the blocking back cheating up

You must be looking for indications of a fake, even when you are in a return defense. We insure against a fake in our returns by having our outside men on both sides pressure the kicker (see Figure 11-4). They join in the return only after the ball is kicked. The pressure also eliminates the kicker holding

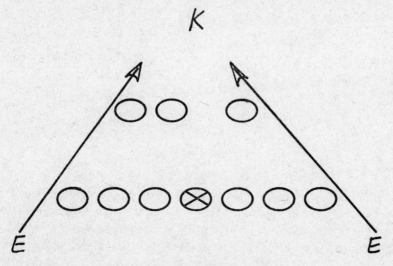

Figure 11-4

the ball to give his coverage more time to get downfield. Some coaches prefer to pressure with only one end. This technique leaves one side vulnerable to the run.

Both end linemen will always come hard when the block is on. Your scouting report will tell you the best location to attempt the block. Similar to extra point blocks, the center should be occupied. You don't want to pass up an opportunity to cause a bad snap.

All block attempts should be designed to take place at the point where the ball will be punted (see Figure 11-5), not at the position of the punter. Attempting the block at the point where the ball is being kicked will reduce the chances of roughing the punter.

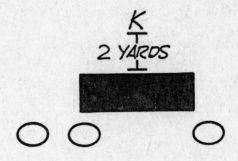

Figure 11-5

When you assign your ends to pressure the punter on returns, be sure to make clear to them whether you want them to go for the block or play safe. Anytime that you are attempting the block, you are in danger of being penalized and losing possession of the ball. This penalty usually occurs when you most desperately need the ball.

We have avoided senseless penalties by telling our pressure men to play soft and not go for the block. The attempt for the block is signaled from the bench. When you do put on the block, be sure that you give assignments for advancing the blocked ball. When you get the block, you should try for the score. This requires a number of additional assignments, other than blocking the punt.

Any time that a punt is blocked on fourth down, your defensive linemen should make an attempt to pick up the ball and advance it. You have nothing to lose by attempting to pick it up because regardless of who recovers it, you will gain possession provided the opponent does not gain the necessary yardage for a first down. If your opponent is punting on third down, the situation is different. If the offense gains control of a blocked punt, they will have the ball for an additional down.

When the punt is blocked, the closest lineman to the ball should pick it up and run with it. The ball should be picked up similar to a fumble, as described in Chapter 10. The yardage gained depends on the reactions of the other defensive linemen. The first opponent that must be blocked is the punter. He is most likely to make the tackle because he feels responsible for the block. After the punter is blocked, defensive linemen must look for opponents coming from the inside.

When the punter is blocked, there is no need to get in front of him because no one will usually be there. Most pursuit will come from the inside. When you don't have a block on, you should take a precaution to insure that you don't give up the ball with an untimely offsides penalty. When your opponent has less than five yards for the first down, you should move your linemen off the ball about three yards to make sure that they are not pulled off-sides on fourth down (see Figure 11-6).

This moving off the ball is especially important late in the game when getting the ball back is crucial. In this situation, you have nothing to gain by being up on the ball, and you risk the possibility of being pulled off-sides.

When you are returning the punt, you can still have your defensive linemen off the ball, but you don't want to sacrifice good contact with the offense. This contact will slow down the

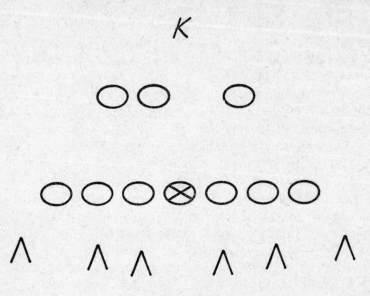

Figure 11-6

opposition's punt coverage and give you an opportunity for a better return.

Facing Field Goals

The field goal attempt must be defended along with the other kicking options. Fake attempts off the field goal are similar to those off the extra point attempt.

On our level of play, most field goal attempts are defended by attempting to block them. Yet, all block attempts must be designed so that they are sound against the pass or run. The pressure applied by the block attempt is usually enough to pressure the fake attempts.

When the field goal attempt is successfully blocked, you should follow the same procedures for advancing the blocked punt. A slight variation is that when the field goal is blocked, the kicker and holder must be blocked first.

Only an unusual situation would dictate a return play on a field goal, but you should be prepared to use it if you need it.

Most high school field goals are never returned because the rules prohibit a ball from being returned from the end zone.

A return could be used at the end of a half or the end of a game when your opponent is attempting a field goal as a last resort and the range is questionable. Also in this situation, you could use a block and a return. This would give you an option if the attempt is not successful.

Reading Audibles

If you know what play the offense is running, you naturally have a better chance to defend it. If you can read some of your opponent's audibles, you increase your chance of knowing what they are going to do.

With audibles, the less frequently they are used, the easier they are to recognize and defend. And since many high school teams don't have more than one or two audibles that they use regularly, you can be fairly certain of what plays the audibles will be when they are called.

Most teams use either a live color or live number to trigger an automatic. Before you find out what color or number is live, you can easily find out what color or number isn't live. In most cases you can eliminate all colors and numbers that you hear used when you scout and the ones that you hear in your opponent's pregame drill.

Live calls that trigger automatics must be made obvious to the offense, and consequently, they are obvious to the defense. Automatics can be recognized by listening to the difference in voice inflection by the quarterback. Your defensive linemen will recognize the difference in voice as "sounding different." Another indicator of an automatic is the live call said twice. Your linemen can pick this up after they get used to hearing all preliminary calls once.

Until you learn to recognize exactly what play the automatic will be, you can expect a basic play such as a quick pass to the tight end, a dive, or a quick pitch. When your linemen recognize an automatic or any other definite offensive key, they should not alert the offense that they know what play is being called. Your alerting signal should alert your team only. This technique will keep the key available longer.

Playing Two-Minute Defense

Another area of defensive football frequently overlooked is the two-minute defense. Offensive coaches prepare to do as much as possible in the last two minutes, but defensive coaches frequently overlook limiting the offense to as little time as possible in those last two minutes.

The idea of a two-minute defense is to use as much time as possible on defense, so the offense has as little time as possible to score. Reducing the offensive time will add additional pressure to an offense that is already pressing to score. In addition, you are forcing the offense to play to your tempo, the normal game tempo, rather than the hurried-up tempo that the offense wants to play.

Generally, you play two-minute defense by using as much time as legally possible between plays. The rules allow you a reasonable amount of time between plays. Frequently, defensive players who are unprepared for two minute defense will actually hurry with the offense to get back into position as quickly as possible. You don't have to hurry.

Specifically, you can legally consume time by performing the following:

1. Taking the normal amount of time to get up from the pile-up of the previous play
2. Walking back to the defensive side of the line of scrimmage, but being prepared for the next play immediately upon reaching the defensive side
3. Trying to keep the clock running as much as possible, including: keeping the ball carrier in bounds, getting the sack, and avoiding the careless penalty

If the offense commits the penalty, the loss of down is frequently more beneficial to you than the loss of yardage.

If you need a time out during the last two minutes, you can

consume additional time by calling time when the offensive team is on the ball and ready to call their play. You can use almost thirty seconds by using the opponent's huddle time and approach time.

We have been successful using another time-consuming technique. It involves our defensive lineman who is away from where the play is run. When our defensive tackle on the end of the line sees the play going away from him, he inconspicuously gets ten to fifteen yards into the opponent's backfield (see Figure 11-7). He stays in the backfield as long as possible, trying to be the last player who returns to the defensive side of the line of scrimmage. If he moves steadily and at a normal pace, the defensive player is within his legal limits. If he moves slowly, he is likely to be called for illegally consuming time.

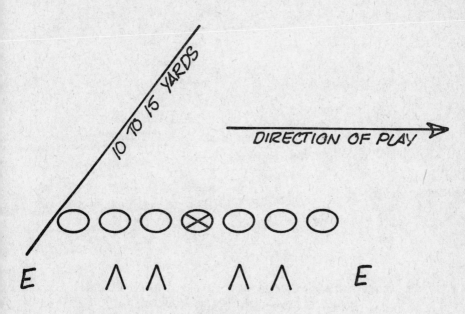

Figure 11-7

All of these techniques will help you use as much time as possible while the offense is trying to use as little as possible.

Psychological Approaches to Defensive Linemen

Because of the nature of the type of person who plays defensive line, they are extremely vulnerable to being psychologically motivated. Often the "psych" of these few players can affect the other members of the team. The listed psychological themes have been successful at our school. They can be used with the whole team or just with the defensive linemen.

The way that the motivational talk is given is almost as important as what is said. The talk should be given in a small area where the players are physically close to one another. Body contact among the players can produce a feeling of electricity.

When you begin your talk, speak softly and slowly. Gradually increase your voice and pace so that at the end of your talk you are speaking loud and fast.

The following themes can be developed to suit your individual needs:

1. We have not yet played our best game . . .
2. All you have to do is stop their offense six times in each half . . .
3. We have to set the tempo with the first series . . .
4. Let us remember each other with this game . . .
5. This is our last game on this field . . .
6. We deserve this game for how hard we work . . .
7. We owe our team a good game . . .
8. We have played our best defensive games against this team . . .

Agility

We are all aware of the importance of having agile defensive linemen. This area of defensive line play is so important that we have specialized drills to develop agility. While there are a myriad of drills available to develop agility, each drill should be designed to develop one or more of three basic areas:

1. Quick hands
2. Quick feet
3. Quick reflexes

We have successfully used a series of agility drills that develop all three. A line of about ten or twelve players lies on the ground like railroad ties (see Figure 11-8). Each player gets off the ground and goes over and in and out of the ties in a manner that develops the three basic areas. They go down and back in the following ways:

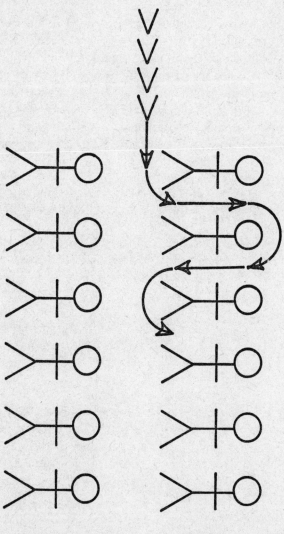

Figure 11-8   Figure 11-9

1. Sprinting with one foot in every space
2. Sprinting with both feet in every space
3. In and out of every space (see Figure 11-9)
4. Sprinting with a cross-over step
5. Backwards
6. Hopping with both feet together

To develop quick hands and reactions, a ball is thrown to every other player as they go through the ties. The players catch the ball and make a return throw to the coach. The complete series of drills doesn't take more than five minutes, and it helps create enthusiasm during an otherwise dull part of practice.

In conclusion, agility is one of the little things that can help give you a big defensive advantage. Developed along with other little areas of defensive line play, your linemen will be well-prepared for almost any situation. By taking care of the little problems, the big ones will be easier to handle.

A big area that you will find easier to handle, if you have a knowledge of little things, is rules. Specific rules that will help you in your coaching of defensive linemen are discussed in Chapter 12.

DRILLS

1. Junk Drill.

Purpose: To condition players to adjust to various junk formations. To teach assignments for junk formations.

Procedure: Offensive team breaks the huddle and aligns in various spread formations (with at least 7 men on the line of scrimmage). The defense reacts according to their junk rules.

Comment: Defensive players sometimes have difficulty distinguishing eligible receivers. In addition to recognizing eligible numbers, the defense should remember that offensive players on both ends of the line are eligible. Adjustments to wide splits can be included in this drill.

2. PAT Drill.

Purpose: To condition players to react to various PAT situations.

Procedure: A defensive team defends against your offensive team's extra points. The offensive team runs the various fakes as the defense defends them.

Comment: Repetition of this drill will condition your defensive players to think trick when they defend extra points.

3. Interception Drill.

Purpose: To teach reaction to and assignments for an interception or other change of possession.

Procedure: Any of the standard interception drills is sufficient.

Comment: The points to be emphasized in any interception drill are the following: reaction to alerting call, quick change to offense, doing not looking, and picking up most critical opponents first.

4. Fourth Down Drill.

Purpose: To condition players to react to various fourth down situations.

Procedure: Use your defense against your punting team. Occasionally, they should run one of the various fourth down fakes.

Comment: If your players are exposed to enough fake situations, they will expect a fake in game situations.

5. Two-Minute Defense Drill.

Purpose: To teach assignments and reactions for defending the last two minutes.

Procedure: Your defensive team defends your two-minute offense.

Comment: The points to be emphasized are discussed in the chapter text.

12

Getting an Edge
from the Rule Book

Being permitted to contact the punter. Encroaching. Avoiding off-sides. Scoring a safety. Advancing a backward pass. Recovering the ball near the sideline. Contacting receivers after a tipped pass. Eliminating blows to the head. Eliminating face-tackling. Getting all you deserve from the umpire. Stopping the clock on defense. Mistakes to avoid when kicking off. Playing a fair catch.

One of the most underestimated areas of our game today is a thorough knowledge of the rule book. We frequently underestimate the kicking game and justify its importance by saying that almost one out of every four plays involves a kicking play—about 25% of the plays of a game. But the area of the rules involves 100% of the plays. This applies not only to the officials' administration of rules, but also to the players' knowledge of what they are allowed to do and what they are not allowed to do.

When you have a thorough knowledge of the rules, officials will be more receptive to listen to you. Officials do an excellent job of administrating our game, but they are human like us and they make mistakes like us. However, if we don't have a thorough understanding of the rules, we will not know when they make a mistake or how to appeal what we are legally entitled to appeal.

The rules discussed in this chapter are from the *Football Rule Book* published by the National Federation of State High School Associations. The National Alliance Edition is endorsed by representatives from every state.

Being Permitted to Contact the Punter

Many rules are critical to the outcome of a game. A rule that you usually encounter in a crucial game situation is roughing the punter. When this call is made late in the game, it usually has a direct influence on the outcome of the game. An understanding of the rule will benefit you and your players.

To understand this rule, you must first realize that under no condition are you allowed to rough the punter. The rule is designed to protect the punter when he is in an awkward and unbalanced position.

Generally, when a defender makes contact with the ball, he is permitted to make contact with the punter. He may not rough the punter, but he may make contact with him in an attempt to block the punt. The punter remains the punter until he has had the opportunity to regain his balance.

If the punter mishandles the pass from center and becomes a runner, he no longer has the protection of the punter and he may be tackled. However, if the runner stops and reestablishes himself as the punter, he is once again afforded the protection of the punter.

Encroaching

Encroachment is another rule that is designed to protect the players. An understanding of the rules can help your defensive linemen eliminate a mental mistake that can cost you five yards—and another player an injury. The rule prohibits any player being in the neutral zone (see Figure 12-1) when the ball is signaled ready for play and after the center has made his final adjustment of the ball.

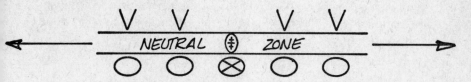

Figure 12-1

This rule means that your defensive signal caller may not be in the neutral zone or make contact with the ball. It also means that if a defensive lineman takes his stance with part of his body in the neutral zone, you are subject to receive a five yard penalty. A few years ago, a defensive player was allowed to line up in the neutral zone, provided he got back before the snap, but that rule was recently changed. Encroachment penalties are blown dead the moment they occur.

Knowledge of the encroachment rule will eliminate your getting a penalty by making a mental mistake and lining up in the neutral zone and also having your signal caller make careless contact with the ball—costing you 5 yards.

Avoiding Off-Sides

Off-sides is similar to encroachment—they are as much mental as physical. A defensive player is off sides when he is illegally in advance of the scrimmage line when the ball is snapped. Defensive linemen usually jump off-side when they listen to the cadence of the quarterback instead of moving on the movement of the offensive linemen.

The cause of going off-sides is usually the lack of concentration. You can temporarily correct jumping off-sides during a game by moving the defensive linemen farther back off the ball.

If a particular player still goes off-sides, you should remove him from the game.

Scoring a Safety

Scoring a safety is an exclusive method for the defense to get points. A safety not only gives a moral boost to the defense, but it also gives the ball back to the offense—usually in good field position.

You can score a safety when:

1. The ball becomes dead in the opponent's end zone.
2. The ball goes out of the opponent's end zone.
3. An illegal forward pass is thrown from the end zone.
4. An offensive player commits a foul which is measured from a spot in the end zone.

Whenever your opponent gives you an opportunity to score a safety, you must be prepared to take advantage of that opportunity. The most obvious opportunity that you have to score a safety is when your opponent has the ball backed up to their end zone. If the ball is spotted inside the one yard line, the snap is actually putting the ball into the end zone and the offense must get it out of the end zone. To score a safety, all you have to do is keep the ball where they snap it. If it were only that easy!

When the offense is backed up to their end zone, they are likely to run sneaks, dives, and other straight basic plays that are designed to gain a few yards. To get the safety, you should play defenses that take away the sneak first and the other basic plays second.

The technique for tackling on these plays is similar to tackling to prevent a score. You want to stop the ball from crossing the plane of the goal line. The hit should be made high so that the ball carrier does not fall forward, out of the end zone.

Anytime the ball is loose in the end zone, your defensive players should first try to recover possession to get six points. If they mishandle the ball and the offense recovers or the ball goes out of the end zone, you will have to settle for two points—and good field position on the ensuing kick off.

To give your team the longest opportunity to get six points, a player who cannot gain control of the ball should try to keep it in the end zone if he cannot gain possession himself. This will give you an additional opportunity to score a touchdown.

Another situation where you can cause a safety is to force the offense to throw an illegal forward pass from their own end zone. An illegal forward pass in this situation would be a pass thrown from the end zone that is intentionally incompleted or that is thrown out of bounds in back of the corner flag.

If you are aware of all these situations, you will be prepared to perform the basic objective of the game—score. You will also be prepared to question an official for what you are entitled.

Advancing a Backward Pass

Another big opportunity for the defense to score is advancing a backward pass. Many times this kind of score can come from a mental lapse. If your defense is prepared for this kind of opportunity, you can get a quick score by advancing the backward pass.

The advancing of the backward pass is often misunderstood by players on the field, and they often confuse it with an incomplete forward pass. Whether the ball is thrown backwards or forwards is a matter of only a few yards, but the result is often six points.

When a pass is in doubt as to whether it is forward or backward, your players should have the philosophy: when in doubt do it. The worst that can happen on an advanced forward pass (incomplete) is that the official will call the play back.

Alert linemen can use the official to trigger reacting to a backward pass. When the ball is thrown backwards, complete or incomplete, the official will not blow the whistle. He will usually stand watching the ball, waiting for the play to continue. The absence of a whistle and the official watching the ball can be a reminder to defensive players to pick up the backward pass and advance it.

Recovering the Ball Near the Sideline

A backward pass or other type of loose ball frequently occurs near the sideline. Many players confuse out-of-bounds possession rules because they vary from sport to sport and your players frequently play other sports.

When a football goes out-of-bounds, it belongs to the team that had possession last—not the team that touched it last. Your players should be aware of that rule when trying to gain possession of a loose ball near the sideline. Frequently, players try to merely touch the ball, instead of controlling it.

Anytime a player goes after the ball near the sideline, he must avoid going out-of-bounds. A player who voluntarily steps out-of-bounds during a play is ineligible to participate in the remainder of that play. If he is knocked out by the opposition, he may return to participate, but not if he goes out on his own.

Another point to remember when going after a loose ball is that the defender may push other players out of the way in an attempt to get to the ball. Your players may actually grab the opponent in an attempt to prevent him from reaching the ball. Knowledge of the rules gives your players maximum opportunity to recover a ball near the sideline.

Contacting Receivers After a Tipped Pass

Another small edge that you can have over your opponent results from a tipped pass. When a pass is tipped (usually behind the line by a defensive player), the defense may make contact with receivers to the extent that pass interference is almost non-existent. Knowing the value of a tip increases the importance of your defensive linemen making contact with a pass.

Your defensive backs can be made aware of the tip by noticing the referee signal a tip with a hand sign—slapping his hands together above his head (like a baseball umpire signaling a foul tip). When the defensive back sees this sign, he should go after the ball with no fear of interfering the receiver. Understanding this tip rule gives your defense an opportunity to play more aggressively.

Eliminating Blows to the Head

We all share the responsibility of making our game as safe as possible. We should be safety conscious in our drills and teaching techniques. We should not teach or suggest a technique that causes a blow to be delivered to the head of the opponent. This is where the opponent changes from an "O" in a diagram to a human being with feelings who is someone's son. Every effort should be made to protect him from injury—especially injuries to the head. Rules in recent years have emphasized eliminating hits to the head, and we have the responsibility to transmit that emphasis to our players.

Eliminating Face-Tackling

Another safety rule that has been emphasized by the rule makers in recent years is face-tackling. The practice of using the head to tackle is dangerous to both the tackler and ball carrier. Serious head and neck injuries have resulted from face-tackling.

Face-tackling and head safety should be a primary consideration when you teach tackling. There are many different methods for teaching this skill. Safety should dictate the technique you teach.

Getting All You Deserve from the Umpire

Occasionally, a defensive player may be illegally prohibited from carrying out his assignment by the actions of an offensive lineman. You and your players may be aware of the illegal action, but you may not know which one of the officials to approach.

Penalties involving holding and other infractions of interior line play are the responsibility of the umpire—the official who is positioned behind the defensive line (see Figure 12-2). When

Figure 12-2

one of your defensive linemen feels that he is being abused by an
offensive lineman, he should quietly approach the umpire and
politely make him aware of what is happening. Your defensive
lineman should mention the number of the offensive player and
what he is doing.

The politeness of your player cannot be overemphasized. If
your player approaches the umpire in a loud and demanding
manner, the official is not likely to listen to him and your player
may be reprimanded. Also, the umpire is not likely to listen to a
player who is frequently accusing an offensive player of constant
abusement. A kind word to the umpire will help you get all you
deserve.

Stopping the Clock on Defense

At some time in almost every game, your defense will be in
a situation where they must not onl get the ball back, but they
must also use as little time as poss ble trying to get it back. Your
defense must know how to stop the clock without using the three
valuable time outs.

In addition to time outs, charged and official, the clock
stops as a result of the following:

1. Out-of-bounds
2. Fair catch
3. Foul

4. Ball going behind the goal line
5. Incompleted forward pass
6. A team attempting to consume time

Some of these situations require special instruction for your defensive linemen to perform effectively. The preparation in these situations is as much mental as physical. An investment in practice time will allow you to have more game time.

Mistakes to Avoid When Kicking Off

Every kick-off gives you an opportunity to put your opponent in poor field position by good coverage and a sure tackle. But to get good coverage, you must eliminate a penalty that can offset a good tackle inside the twenty—off-sides.

A defensive player is off-sides on the kick-off when he breaks the plane of the ball before it is kicked. Linemen on your kick-off team must be quick enough to be at the ball when the kicker makes contact and smart enough to be behind it when it is kicked.

This specialty area of the game requires the practice timing of an offensive play. Ten players must coordinate their speed with the approach of the kicker. If the kicker is slow approaching the ball, ten players can easily be off-sides. Changing kickers is similar to replacing a center or quarterback—timing must be re-adjusted.

Another mistake to avoid when kicking off is kicking the ball out-of-bounds. When the ball is kicked out-of-bounds, the opponent gets possession of the ball on their 40 yard line. You are giving them a 30-40 yard return. (American Federation Rules)

A consistent kicker from the middle of the field will usually keep the ball in play, but be sure to make adjustments when you kick from one of the hash marks. When you place the ball on the hash mark, you are less than 18 yards from the sideline. A slice from this position can easily result in a forty yard gain for your opponent. A few minutes invested in your kick-off coverage can return a dividend of many yards.

Playing a Fair Catch

Another part of the kicking game that is often misunderstood is the fair catch. A thorough understanding of the fair catch rules will help your defense and your offense.

When your punt team is covering the ball, they should be prepared to take advantage of any opportunity given by the opposition. Many opportunities come as a result of the receiving team calling a fair catch. When your team is covering a fair catch, they should take one look to see the direction of the ball so that they avoid being hit by the ball and avoid a penalty.

We like to have our first man downfield run past the catcher in an attempt to distract his concentration on the ball. The other defenders should *expect* the catcher to miss the ball. Once the signaler touches the ball, he must catch it. A missed fair catch is a loose ball and anyone is entitled to it. If the fair catch is muffed (touched, but not possessed), the punting team can recover it but may not advance it.

A fair catch signal gives the receiver protection to catch the ball at the expense of forfeiting his right to run. A valid signal is "extending and laterally waving one arm only, at full arm's length above the head." A variation of this signal is a violation.

Offensively, you receive the following benefits when you call a fair catch:

1. The clock stops
2. The right to snap the ball anywhere between the hash marks
3. The right to a free kick

A free kick gives you the right to line up for a kick (from the yard line of the fair catch) in an attempt to kick the ball between the goal posts for 3 points.

The free kick option is seldom used, but you should be thinking about it anytime your opponent is kicking from deep in their own territory. To prepare for the free kick, you should do it in practice and know the range of your kick-off man.

In conclusion, rules are one of the many important parts of making a defensive lineman complete. If you want your defensive linemen to be well prepared, you must prepare them well.

DRILLS

Preparing players to understand rules is as much mental as physical. In addition to drilling specific rule situations, we devote a pre-season meeting to the explanation of rules. We discuss rules that are applicable to the players. The discussion is followed by a question and answer period and then a written test. The following is a sample of the true/false test we give to our players.

1. If you touch the ball, you may rough the punter.
2. If the punter begins to run, he can no longer regain the protection of the punter.
3. Roughing the punter is an automatic first down.
4. If you line up off-sides, you may get back before the ball is snapped.
5. An illegal forward pass thrown from the end zone is a safety.
6. An incomplete backward pass is a dead ball.
7. The team that last touches the ball before it goes out-of-bounds is entitled to get possession of it.
8. The back judge has the main responsibility for watching interior line infractions.
9. The clock stops on a fair catch.
10. A player who signals for a fair catch may not block if he decides not to catch the ball.
11. A fair catch gives you the right to attempt a free kick for three points.
12. Any player on the team may signal a fair catch.
13. If a piece of equipment breaks, a player should ask the official for a charged time out.
14. Pass interference is an automatic first down.
15. Defensive players must make a definite effort to avoid charging into a passer after it is clear that the ball has been thrown.
16. The ball is dead and play is stopped whenever the whistle is sounded, even though it may be inadvertent.

17. If the kick-off is kicked out-of-bounds, the kicking team rekicks. (American Federation Rules)

18. A substitute is required to leave the field on the side on which his team box is located.

19. The chin strap does not have to be fastened.

20. A touchdown is scored when the ball touches the ground in the end zone.

Answers: 1. F, 2. F, 3. T, 4. F, 5. T, 6. F, 7. F, 8. F, 9. T, 10. F, 11. T, 12. T, 13. F, 14. T, 15. T, 16. T, 17. F, 18. T, 19. F, 20. F.

Index